W9-BDA-770

NEVER AGAIN

Learning from America's
Foreign Policy Failures

*For my father
Alan M. Ravenal*

NEVER AGAIN

Learning from America's
Foreign Policy Failures

EARL C. RAVENAL

Temple University Press PHILADELPHIA

Library of Congress Cataloging in Publication Data
Ravenal, Earl C.
  Never again.
  1. United States—Foreign relations—1945-
2. United States—Foreign relations—1977-
I. Title.
JX1417.R38   327.73   77-91392
ISBN 0-87722-107-3 cloth
ISBN 87722-187-1 paper

Temple University Press, Philadelphia 19122
© 1978 by Temple University. All rights reserved
Published 1978
Printed in the United States of America
Paperback edition published 1980.

Intervention Revived

"Afghanistan"—the swift, brutal Soviet invasion of that country, in December 1979, to install a complaisant regime and put down a host of rebellions against the Marxist central government—may have resulted in the revival of interventionism in the United States. Has it also destroyed the logic of the non-interventionist position?

In the hard cover edition of this book, published in the fall of 1978, I said that more important than the experience of Vietnam would be how America learned its lessons. The early signs were that the nation had learned little—at least little that was correct, coherent, effective, and durable. Indeed, it had derived many diverse and false lessons, that would afflict American foreign policy for decades to come.

Some were "instrumental" lessons, to the effect that we could, and should, do better "next time"—and there were to be many next times. The critique of the doves, who ad-

hered mostly to the "proportionalist" camp, was especially
portentous: They believed that Vietnam was an avoidable
mistake and that they could distinguish the good from the
bad wars, they were not necessarily reluctant to fight the
"good" ones, and this would be an unreliable principle to
prevent future disasters. The "consequential" argument,
that defense spending distorts priorities and starves the
public domestic sector, has been seen most recently in the
so-called "transfer amendments" (arbitrary shifts of defense funding to domestic needs—as if each sector lacked
its own requirements, whatever they might be). The argument of the "fundamentalists"—the moralists and the
ideologues of the left—was powerful but finally irrelevant
to the strategic challenges of the future, which would be
decided on strategic grounds—that is, in terms of the capabilities and interests of the United States in a world of
changing and increasingly tight parameters.

In any event, I judged that what would matter is not so
much what various people thought about intervention,
but the existential lessons of the Vietnam era—the actual
residue that became imbedded in our institutions and
behavior: such items as the volunteer army, the tax revolt,
the creation of more tailored intervention forces, the
preparation for waging more technological and antiseptic
war.

"Afghanistan" has, I think, validated these observations
and judgments. What remains in this introduction is to
evaluate the problems of the present and the policies of
the Carter administration in a spirit that is compatible with
the analysis of the original book.

A Winter's Tale

There's a nice scene in "The Godfather" where one of
the headstrong sons wants to confront a rival with some
proposition and the old Don cautions him. "Mention it,
don't insist." That would also have been good advice for
America in the aftermath of Afghanistan, as an eerie

euphoria swept this country, like the one that inflamed Europe in August 1914. Don Vito's counsel didn't betoken cowardice—just healthy realism and an interest in staying alive for a while.

The significance of "Afghanistan" was extensively canvassed in editorials, journals of opinion, and political speeches over the winter of 1979-80. And even as Afghanistan itself has faded again into the tapestry of general Soviet pressure, this country has continued to debate its implications for our foreign and military policy. But curiously—or perhaps understandably—one position has hardly been expounded: non-intervention. That is, the case for doing nothing. Not symbolic measures, not oblique retaliations, not vague threats, not verbal doctrines, not basing and deployment schemes, but flat nothing.

The one thing that almost anyone (doves as well as hawks, liberals and conservatives alike) would say about Afghanistan is that we can't "just sit on our hands." I wonder: Why not? That sounds precisely like what we ought to be doing. If we can't prudently do something that is directly helpful—for example, free Afghanistan immediately, painlessly, costlessly, risklessly, from Soviet occupation—then we should be making the least of it, not the most. And if we can't defend the Persian Gulf from halfway around the world; if all we have, in the first resort as well as the last resort, is the threat of blowing up the planet, then we should be hedging against the deprivation of oil, not planning to start a world war.

These are times that try the souls of non-interventionists. The spectrum of ordinary opinion is divided: the triumphant hawks, the chastened doves, only recently converted to fear and bellicose reaction; and the other doves, the left-liberal remnant, embarrassed by the erosion of the factual basis of their position and straining to find another benign formula for avoiding a final slide into intervention. Worse, perhaps, than the vindictive hawks are the repentant doves, who feel personally outraged at the Russians for mocking their earlier notions of how the world works. "Betrayed, yes, that's the word," complains Senator Ed Muskie. Russia "just ran out on us." George Ball, the old reliable devil's advocate of "hopeful" diplomatic solutions, now wants bigger defense budgets, more airlift, sealift, Marines, and bases throughout the Middle East; revival of the draft, and urgent coercion of Israel into a settlement favoring pan-Islamic goals. Clark Clifford, who wisely persuaded Lyndon Johnson to abandon Vietnam, is peddling American arms, and threats, around South Asia. The sunshine non-interventionists (those who, by the 1970s, had acquired the wisdom and the courage to oppose the "bad war" in Vietnam) have turned, with Afghanistan as a pretext. One summer, it seems, does not make a dove; and a few doves don't make a summer.

Putative critics strain at gnats to delineate some difference in their go-along positions and the "Carter Doctrine." Here is an editorial in the *New Republic* entitled "Steady, Big Fella" (February 16, 1980): "We support many of the specific policies that make up Carter's born-again approach to the Soviet Union, but we are profoundly worried by the mindset that produced them—the emotionalism, the inconsistency, the moralism, the excessive swings in the president's mood from pacific euphoria to euphoric militance. . . . What the United States needs is a steady vision . . . [etc., etc.] . . . leadership—prudent and resolute leadership. . . ."

To document the point further, here is Anthony Lewis, writing on the *New York Times* Op-Ed page (February 14, 1980), qualifying his opposition to the Carter Doctrine, supporting the moves but striving to maintain an intellectual fig leaf of proportion and selectivity. "Americans have reason for concern about the Soviet occupation of Afghanistan, and reason to act against the potential threat to the Persian Gulf. But the action should be related to the threat. Demonstrations of a commitment in the Gulf, refusals to carry on business as usual with the Soviets and, most important, action to reduce our dependence on oil from the region: These are the kinds of steps that make sense. What does not make sense—what will indeed drain our economic and psychological strength—is undifferentiated militarism . . . a blank check . . . hysteria. . . ."

There we have it, the liberal syndrome: applaud the presidential actions, decry the emotive aura and the nasty language. Some may recall similar critical noises that enveloped the Truman Doctrine in 1947: We needed the response, the commitment, but heavens! the indiscriminate rhetoric, the "universalism," the anti-communist "hysteria," the "blank check," the "mindset" that produced it. I would agree that the new policy would eventually lead to Korea, Dullesian brinkpersonship (I suppose you'd now have to call it), Kennedy's "finest hour" of near-extinction in the Cuban missile crisis, and finally Vietnam—but not because of all that dirty language in the Truman Doctrine; rather because this country had been set, in so many tangible ways, on an interventionist track, and every successive challenge had a certain irresistibly attractive aspect. That interventionist logic is what is being set in place again, now that the post-Vietnam debate appears to be resolving —or dissolving—into a fine belligerent froth. And we are seeing again the same parade of inconsequential critical nonsense, the vain attempt to maintain editorial credibility in a rising sea, not so much of "hysteria"—though we have that too—but of foolish policies and dangerous actions.

Carter vs. Carter

Jimmy Carter is also a converted dove. His State of the Union message in January 1980 should have been billed as "Carter vs. Carter," since the President testified against the foreign policy of the first three years of his own administration. That policy had been non-interventionist, not through principle or design, but by indirection and default. At Notre Dame in May 1977, the administration was going to select new priorities—North-South instead of East-West, cosmic optimism instead of Spenglerian gloom, rampant moralism instead of cynical Realpolitik. The United States was summoned to give up its "inordinate fear of communism"—to have it replaced, as it turned out, with a sort of *ordinate* fear of communism. Foreign policy bureaucrats could put Soviet relations on the "back burner." Internal policy documents such as "PRM-10" proclaimed the advent of an "Era Two," in which we could presumably cash in our spiritual superiority for strategic advantage, define ourselves into another world. We could declare that we won the Cold War and quit.

But "revising priorities" is not foreign policy-making; it is speech-writing. In foreign policy, you don't revise priorities. You dispose your system to respond in some real way to possible challenges. And challenges there will be, but you can't determine—let alone dictate—what kind, from what quarter, how serious, how insistent; that is for the challengers, and they have their own priorities.

There was the first hint of nervous bellicosity in the presidential speech of March 1978 (delivered, appropriately, at Winston-Salem since Carter sounded like a tobacco man, not a medicine man). And there was the two-toned incoherence of the draft Carter read at Annapolis in July 1978, offering the Soviets a bit of confrontation and a bit of cooperation too.

The result was a sort of catatonic inaction. The clinical definition of catatonia, by the way, is: "a syndrome seen most frequently in schizophrenia, with muscular rigidity and mental stupor, sometimes alternating with great excitement and confusion." Some would say that still sounds like an apt characterization of the foreign policy of the Carter administration. But if we can't have deliberate and consistent non-intervention, we must be grateful for incompetence, paralysis, and the babel of many tongues.

Perhaps we should not be too surprised by the conversion of the Carter administration. The liberals sooner or later become the executors of the foreign and military policies of the Right—though always, they assure us, reluctantly, and always earning the contempt of the hawks for their pains.

All of the Above

But what has "Afghanistan" done? Contrary to the belief and hope of the hawks, the egregious Soviet conduct has not invalidated the case for non-intervention. Afghanistan has simply stripped the veils from arguments that have passed for non-interventionist but were really evasions of choice or, worse, closet prescriptions for selective intervention. Indeed, the I-told-you-so hawks profit in their selection of targets: the guilt-ridden moralists and revisionist historians, who impugned so uniquely the motives of American leaders; the exotic exegetes of three decades of Russian behavior, who explained it as merely a lagged response to American strategic provocation; those who pronounced the Soviet Union a "status quo power," presumably so bloated and torporous after its thirty-year global lunch that it could hardly rouse itself for another course, the purveyors of Pickwickian definitions of "security" that failed to include any defensive component.

Most of those arguments would interpret "the threat" out of existence. In the case of Afghanistan, to those who asserted that the Soviets were pursuing their traditional push toward warm water ports and who saw them positioning themselves along the flanks of the West's oil lifeline, the others replied that they were just "rounding out a belt of satellites" or quelling Moslem unrest that could spill over into their own backyard. If some took Afghanistan as a token of Russia's inexorable quest for world dominance, the others insisted that it was merely an expression of Russia's continuing paranoia. Some said that Moscow's move reflected a tendency to exploit unrest along its borders, but the others judged that the Soviets did no more than we did fifteen years ago in Vietnam.

Actually, the "right" answer might be: all of the above. But does it matter? I would be impertinent enough to suggest that discerning the sources of this season's Soviet conduct doesn't prove a thing. We are faced with the unfortunate coincidence that the countries that lie in Russia's path also happen to be part of a brittle crust of territory that we could plausibly have a war about.

What matters, rather, is *our own* propensity to intervene, regardless of whether our intervention is holy or profane, whether we are welcomed or not, whether our aid is begged or disdained. What matters also is our own calculus of intervention—whether or not it is feasible within the constraints that beset our system and pervade the international system. In these respects the judgment of our recent experience remains that intervention is likely to be expensive, risky, and fruitless—not in all cases, to be sure, but generally enough so that the whole enterprise should not be undertaken.

The hawks have greeted the defections of the summer non-interventionists as proof that the nation is belatedly emerging from its comatose reaction to Vietnam—that "trauma," that "failure of nerve." But they miss the point. The real lessons of Vietnam are not the data of misplaced pop psychology; they are the things Vietnam proved about our system: the capabilities, the constraints (which are, in the last analysis, social and constitutional); its ability to respond, to persevere, to deliver sustained support to political authorities in obscure, intractable, precarious conflicts; how much grace we will give our leaders to make good on their promises before we politically emasculate another president. These are objective matters and cannot be casually or willfully set aside; and they tell whether an American president can credibly wield the threat of military intervention.

Deals

Some critics—generally within the left-liberal segment of the spectrum—reflecting on America's strategic predicament and their own logical predicament, have been led to benign and right-minded but essentially wishful calls for a new deal with the Russians, new rules of the game.[1] Sure, deals . . . but what would they consist of? Any imaginable starting point would be *post*-Afghanistan (some would call that the "someday-Monsieur-you-go-too-far" position); and the end would be a crass condominium of the two superpowers. They would be Nixon-Kissinger-type deals, to wit. We let you run your part of the world, you let us run ours. And we would still need the threat of American force to make them stick.

Actually, there's nothing particularly new about deals. Nixon and Kissinger thought they had a deal with the Russians, in Moscow 1972 and San Clemente 1973; it didn't last much beyond the Mideast war of October 1973. And the obsession with impressing upon our adversaries certain "codes" of conduct has, from the start, characterized the approach of Zbigniew Brzezinski: "What we have to establish is that the rules of the game have to be the same for both sides." (Interview by Elizabeth Drew, *The New Yorker*, May 1, 1978.) The kind of deal envisaged by Brzezinski inevitably incorporates the aspect of linkage—the contrived relation of various functional categories of the adversary's behavior and the American response: the balance of strategic nuclear forces, political and military ambitions in other regions of the world, trade and investment and technology, the practice of human rights. Several administrations have been looking for ways to multiply linkages in order to re-establish American control over the conduct of other nations. The Carter administration first repudiated, then espoused linkage, but with a twist that reversed the emphasis of the Nixon-Kissinger regime. Nixon and Kissinger had attempted to entangle the Soviets in a web of useful commercial contacts that would not easily be broken for the sake of strategic opportunism. Carter and Brzezinski turned linkage from a carrot into a stick.

I say the less linkage the better. In a world interlaced

with risks of nuclear destruction, where geopolitics is becoming a prohibitively expensive game, we should be looking for ways to *de*-link: to minimize provocations; to let regional conflicts burn themselves out; to suppress commitments engendered by alliances (which, correctly seen, are not barriers to war but transmission belts for war); to "decouple" one stage of escalation from another, cutting the chain from conventional war to a strategic nuclear exchange; to compartmentalize the world's troubles, for there will be many. We should de-link international functions, such as trade, communications, cultural affairs, and yes, even sports, from matters of "high strategy." Indeed, we should keep "the national interest" out of the affairs of citizens and their private organizations. On both sides of the cold war, cliques that call themselves governments presume that they can appropriate and manipulate the activities of those who happen to live within their borders.

My formula would not exclude such specific and delimited compacts as a strategic arms limitation treaty. The case for SALT—though never perfectly satisfying—is actually stronger now, objectively. The less we can trust others' conduct, the more we need a yardstick to calibrate it. But the best strategic moves are those we could make independently, to curtail expensive, destabilizing weapons systems such as the MX land-based missile and the long-range cruise missiles. Such moves must make sense on their own terms; and if they do, we don't need Russian reciprocity.

With respect to American allies and clients, this is my prescription: disengagement for us, self-reliance for others. Others seem to understand this, much better than Americans. One who is in the line of fire is President Zia-ul-Haq of Pakistan. He well knows that those who might have depended on the United States must now make up deficiencies in their own defensive posture, and perhaps simultaneously make some intelligent accommodation with powerful neighbors: "Given the new power equation in the world, self-reliance will be the key to our survival as a nation. . . . If you have to live in the sea, says an old proverb, you have to learn to live with the whales." (*Newsweek*, January 14, 1980). Accordingly, Zia spurned the belated, desperately proffered American military aid package.

Finally, if we cannot dominate the present sources of our economic necessities, particularly energy, we must be prepared to substitute, to tide over, to ride out other countries' political manipulation of resources. But, contrary to the wisdom of many who are friendly to the non-interventionist position, this should not mean central "planning" and coerced conservation. We should allow our private commercial organizations to deal abroad as long as they are able, on whatever business terms they can get, commodity by commodity. And we should take advantage of the flexibility and intelligence that markets (even partially rigged markets) can provide, and the relatively smooth adjustments that the price mechanism can help to mediate.

In short, the trick is to learn to live in a world *without* deals, without rules an asymmetrical world, an unfair world, if you will. Bleak as it may sound, we should observe a code of conduct that is constructive for ourselves, even if it is not reciprocated. For the key to a policy of non-intervention that is consistent enough to withstand a few tests by the Soviets and others in the months and years to come is acceptance of the costs of non-intervention.

Political Pornography

It's strange that the self-described "hardliners" rarely resort to equally hard data about the costs—and thus the attractiveness and feasibility—of the strategic moves they urge upon the American people. Never any numbers; with them it is all nouns, adjectives, and verbs—psychological metaphors, epic poetry, Norman Podhoretz's "undifferentiated fear, loathing, and revulsion," "native anti-Ameri-

canism," "self-hatred," and the like. Literary critics have
become our mentors, our chaplains and confessors, in matters of national security and resource allocation.

But the real argument has always been about the requisites of peace in a nuclear age—more precisely, about how
we can gain for ourselves an interval of peace in an age of
worldwide political, social, and economic chaos, but also
an age of nuclear parity and nuclear "plenty" (to use
Kissinger's perversely appealing term). Those who search
for these requisites of peace are not therefore a bunch of
finks and faggots—as Podhoretz slyly intimated two years
ago, in an article called "The Culture of Appeasement"
(*Harper's*, October 1977) that has become a modern classic
of political pornography.

I would not want to bat at that pathological wicket. The
obsession with "culture" misses all the critical features of
the situation, not just the strategic ones but the truly
moral ones as well. What is relevant is not culture but
structure. That is, "isolationism" *is* the point, but the concept has to be endowed with more tangible meaning and
more contemporary significance. It means, first, that we
might have to "let" some countries be dominated, in the
next decade or so, by our adversaries or their supposed
proxies. And then, we might have to tell some importunate
clients that they are on their own, that they will have to
muster what internal support and scrape up what other
external support they can to repel attack and repress
subversion.

This may not be a very sympathetic position to hold.
But the essential word in this formulation is not any of
the long ones; it is the word "let." For if anything must
change—if anything is in fact changing—it is the ability of
the United States to do something effective about the rest
of the world, and the presumption that we ought to do
something to prevent one kind of outcome and promote
another. That, I think, is the structural significance of
what our false elites diagnose as a disease of the American

spirit. And that is why the problems we face at this historic juncture are even more substantial, and the real alternatives are even more stark, than are posited by the sponsors of the new American Kulturkampf (there! at least one of those words can be spelled with a "k").

Rust or Explode

Who will still argue, "after Afghanistan," for a smaller military force and a reduced defense budget? Even Geroge Kennan, whose sage (and safe) call for "mature statesmanship" was so gratefully received, hastens to grant the hawks the only practical measure of ability and intent: "These words are not meant to express opposition to a prompt and effective strengthening of our military capabilities relevant to the Middle East." As for the "big stick," he asks, "who could object?" Well, I could, for one. The case for military reductions is no worse than it was five years ago, when it was a lot more respectable and the defense budget was a lot lower; it isn't the Russians that have changed. And the case for arms expansion is no better now, suddenly, than it ever was. There are still only two things weapons can do: rust or explode; and we must pray that they rust.

What are the costs of defending these new areas of American commitment—Southwest Asia, the Indian Ocean, and the Persian Gulf—against Soviet penetration and interdiction? How do they fit into the larger pattern of American strategic expenditure? And how do we get a "handle" on this relationship? First of all, the defense budget request of the Carter administration for fiscal year 1981 is $159 billion. At least partially "because of" Afghanistan and related challenges, the only debate in sight, with regard to this and future defense budgets, is between the five-percenters and the eight- or ten-percenters. Just an average of these tendencies, on top of a plausible expectation of inflation, gives us 20 percent annual increases—a defense budget of $329 billion by 1985, and over eight hundred billion dollars a year by the end of the decade. We already spend from $25 to 30 billion a year to support our interests in the Middle East.

A strange thing has been happening to me lately, in presenting these kinds of figures—which might be taken as a token of the changing times. I find myself challenged by the hawks to spell out the costs of *non*-intervention—in effect to specify the costs of peace. Now I don't mind the burden of proof, but I don't know why the *unique* burden should be on those who would avoid war, to prove that we won't lose anything or that we can stand the loss of whatever the hawks are urging us to fight for. Presumably the hawks believe that deterrence is perfect so there won't be any costs of war, and that deterrence is free (a sort of "public good") so the incremental costs of war preparation will be zero. They would take every plausibly threatened country, every possible loss of American interests—trade, investment, strategic position—sum them up, and multiply by a probability of 1.0 (that is, the certainty of total loss if we failed to defend).

To be fair, why shouldn't we throw the costs of war and war preparation into the balance against the costs of what we might lose if we failed to defend and "the worst" happened? On one side, aggressive deterrence—say, the Carter Doctrine or even more—and the chance of a minor regional war and a major nuclear war besides, plus the constant costs, year in and year out, of additional defense preparations, on the other side, the chance of a Soviet invasion or a Soviet-sponsored coup, followed by the denial of oil and other materials. On both sides, you have monstrously large amounts, in the tens of trillions of dollars, multiplied by absurdly small percentages of probability. You are comparing, really, not precise quantities but orders of magnitude.

Nevertheless I did some rough calculations. Surprisingly, the costs of war and the costs of peace come out about the same. Just for the record: I figured defense preparations as an additional eight percent real cost a year, compounded, for twenty years; and that comes to $587 billion. That's the easy part. Now, the costs of a possible war if we deny the region to the Russians—both a regional conventional war and escalation to central nuclear war. The small, limited war for a start: A plausible accounting basis would be Vietnam, which cost about $450 billion (give or take $100 billion or so) including pensions and debt interest; multiply that by a 10 percent increase in the probability of war if we bar the path of the Russians, and you get $45 billion. Plus the big war: In a nuclear war, we might lose half our gross national product—that is, lose about $1¼ trillion a year, on the average, for twenty years—a total of about $25 trillion, multiplied by an incremental probability of perhaps two percent (and here I err generously on the side of the hawks) if we were to threaten escalation to nuclear war, you come out at half a trillion dollars for the "expected damage" of a nuclear war. (I'm not discounting to present value the costs of war; that's all "in the noise level.")

Now you have to measure all this against the losses we might incur by default—assuming that the Soviets invaded, say, Saudi Arabia and the other oil-producing Gulf states; that the invasion was successful; and further that the Soviets deprived the West of these resources indefinitely. Of course, we should really discount these assumptions, for the reluctance to invade even if given a clear field, the possible failure to overcome the defense and absorb the victim country, the fact that the Russians' new clients might not be so stringent in their trade policies toward the West, the probability that we could adjust somehow, and the projection that even if we didn't adjust we would not be so badly damaged. But, even assuming the worst, a plausible shorthand for all the damage might be that we would lose 20 percent of our gross national product for 20 years (and that, too, is an extreme overestimate, another concession to the hawks). That would yield, out of a GNP of $2½ trillion, ½ trillion dollars a year; times twenty years it comes to $10 trillion; and that times an incremental probability of even 10 percent yields an "expected loss" of about one trillion dollars.

To sum it up, you have: (1) standing up to the Russians —an incremental cost of $587 billion for additional defense preparations plus "expected losses" of $45 billion for a regional conventional war and $500 billion for a nuclear war, a total of $1.132 trillion; (2) defaulting—nonintervention, the "appeasement" scene—an expected price tag of about $1 trillion. So, when you get through figuring the "expected losses"—that is, losses cut by probability— you have between 1 and 1½ trillion dollars either way, war or peace.

But what does it prove? Not much. In the last analysis, the costs are incommensurate: One way, we edge perceptibly closer to the devastation of nuclear war; the other way, we may invite circumstances in the distant future where we live less well—but live. The casualties of the general nuclear war might be 125 million Americans; and the casualties of even the conventional regional war might be 50,000 to 100,000. But one way we might be colder and poorer, the other way we would be a lot warmer—in fact rather toasty—and we'd lose the oil anyway, and much, much more.

Naturally, there are some important intangibles that attach to the choice of peace or war. If we were to insist on peace even at the cost of appearing to default on our commitments, there would be the defection of some clients from our security protection, the dissolution of alliances, the loss of American control, a "looser" international system. That could be unnerving—if it weren't happening anyway as surely as the law of entropy. On the other side, the preparation for war will be costly, in private and public welfare foregone, constitutional processes distorted, citizens and their assets mobilized, bodies and minds regimented. Those costs are borne year in and year out, whether this or that intervention is a quagmire or a piece of cake.

Isolationism

One of the bizarre items in the sociology of foreign policy is that so many manifestations of American opinion are labeled "isolationist." That has to be some kind of a sick joke; because the *only* position that is instantly unpopular, that is routinely suppressed by the media, that can't be aired in "responsible" forums, is "isolationism"—that is, consistent, principled non-interventionism. Non-intervention is casually, reflexively scapegoated by such guardians of forensic purity as the editorial staff of the *New York Times*. As it commends President Carter's "warning and new military preparations, including draft registration," the *Times* intones a prayer of thanksgiving that "the gas lines, the Teheran hostages and now Afghanistan have roused many Americans to the dangers of profligate oil consumption and foolish isolationism." (February 17, 1980.)

But the logic of non-intervention is ill-understood, even by those who are assailed by the defense claque for their pusillanimity. Those "ex-Carter aides," those "closet McGovernites" of the overheated imagination of Evans and Novak, those recent waves of boat people fleeing the newly pugnacious administration, the losers of the Special Olympics of bureaucratic rivalry (the only Olympics we're going to get this year) still speak in carefully hedged codewords, either so shallow or so contradictory as to be inconsequential for hard policy choice or contingent national action. In a typical statement,[2] they decry the "emotional pursuit of security through military means." They would include "economic, political and diplomatic *as well as military* components." In fact, they approve all manner of military measures—conventional forces, lift, instruments of deterrence—as long as these do not qualify as "massive." They do not deny security threats, only the "oversimplified view of security threats."

What does all this counter-rhetoric entail? Either nothing or anything—and that's just the trouble. It is posturing

—or, in the parlance of Madison Avenue, "positioning"—
not policy. It is not non-interventionism, let alone "isolationism." Indeed, the trouble with the quasi-non-interven-
tionists, and the source of their inevitable conversion, the
reason their arguments wither or freeze or whatever in the
plains and hills of an Afghanistan, is not that they are too
isolationist, but that *they are not isolationist enough.*

Not so long ago—and perhaps still, in the twilight of
liberal policy analysis—one could win points by positing
an important distinction, and consequently an essential
choice, between the politics of "primacy" and the politics
of "world order." First year law students might call this a
distinction without a difference. In fact, the kind of "world
order" congenial to the liberal internationalists, the "managed interdependence" cherished by the would-be global
architects of Council on Foreign Relations study groups,
depends on the assertion of American primacy. Indeed, it
is virtually synonymous with it, though sometimes attrac-
tively disguised by a few "North-South" tassels and a bit
of "world's commons" embroidery. Making a common
cause out of other people's business not only justifies but
promotes intrusive and even aggressive state conduct.

That should bring us to a sense of our real choices at
this poignant moment. It is easy to note, and regret,
America's defeats and defaults of the past decade. It is
harder to see that, in the aftermath of "Afghanistan" (the
emblem for the half-dozen or dozen challenges and probes
that America has fielded and fumbled), the comfortable
middle options have dropped away. We are left with the
classic dilemma of the mature imperial power (not that
America is "imperial" in the pejorative sense of the revisionist historians; we never behaved quite like that, though
we are not much better off for having been relatively restrained and certainly reactive). The liberals had better
stop calling names, because the only alternative now to the
official strategy of resuscitated military interventionism—
as the Administration lapses into Cold War II (or into a

cold war that really never ended)—is an "isolationist" foreign policy.

Adjustment

The largest question in the desultory, inconclusive public debate we are now having—that "great debate," disguised as often as represented by a succession of surrogate issues— is whether time and situation have outrun the thirty-year American foreign policy paradigm of deterrence and alliance, and whether a new orientation might be demanded. This would have to be an entirely new paradigm—a counter-paradigm—not just another oscillation within the old one.

Actually, a "methodological" issue is at stake here. We would adjust our policies to evolving circumstances and shifting parameters, rather than try to shape those circumstances and move those parameters—or to affect the luxury of avoiding them. We would ask a different kind of question: Not whether intervention is justified in terms of American interests. Of course it sometimes is. But that is increasingly beside the point. We have to ask whether the object of our intervention is part of the irreducible core of our security. If it is, then I suppose we have "no choice." But if we can live without something—and most situations, on cool reflection, are in this category—then we have to evaluate the costs and benefits of intervention, not just in that specific case, but more generally the costs of maintaining in perpetuity the means to execute interventions across a whole spectrum of technology and geography, since challenges will not occur in convenient forms and convenient places. And, like the Alcoholics Anonymous prayer, we had better begin to recognize which situations are which, even if that implies getting some extraterrestrial guidance.

When we look at America's situation in this way—in terms of the objectives and constraints—we see that the cost-benefit ratio of attempts at control is tilting: It is costing more to achieve less. And the domestic acceptability ratio—the costs and sacrifices and risks measured against the extent and probability of foreseen gains—is also tilting, in the opposite direction: The public will not pay as much, even if promised the same results.

The policies and actions of state are the output of our total system, not the imagined or promised responses of a handful of elites that purport to represent that system. Ordinary Americans might make some initial errors in reposing trust in and delegating power to their leaders; but they are constantly evaluating the question of whether the game is worth the candle. Not whether it is worth playing at all, in some absolute sense, but whether it is worth the requisite candle-power. The underlying question about "foreign" policy in our time is, therefore, whether American leaders can count on their own people to generate this candle-power—and not in placid and untested moments, but in critical moments of challenge and stress.

That is why accusations of "failure of nerve" and invocations of "will" are so shallow and misleading. "Will" is not something foreign policy players can summon and shape and project, but is the complex of domestic constraints, which are not subject to their control at all. These domestic constraints, in the last analysis, are as "foreign" and inaccessible as the recalcitrant behavior of other countries.

"Peace for our Time"

There is no doubt that the non-interventionist cause suffers from a lack of appealing labels. But let's be honest about it: Non-intervention *does* borrow from such antecedents as "isolationism" (if this is understood as disengagement), "Fortress America" (what else?), "America First" (now that was a coalition—from Norman Thomas to Charles Lindbergh), even Neville Chamberlain's "peace for our time" (how much worse is that than Richard Nixon's "generation of peace"? and Afghanistan, too, is a "a far-off country about which we know nothing").

In his celebrated diatribe on appeasement, Norman Pod-horetz said: "I have been struck very forcibly by certain resemblances between the United States today and Great Britain in the years after the first world war." He reckoned, in that temporal analogy the hawks use as a benchmark of our own situation, that we had reached "1937." Two years later, if we have really reached "1939," we should re-think World War II, not prepare to fight World War III. You don't have to consider the Russians as cute kola bears; just imagine Hitler with nukes. Who would fight and who would negotiate? Who would be the villains and who the heroes? The brave and the dead? Who would be ready to put 125 million of his fellow citizens' lives on the line to defend his own "values"? Maybe what we need now is a King and Country Oath for the 1980s.

But if we have to find more positive images for non-interventionism, maybe we should call it a kind of realism, even national maturity, in an evolving strategic universe. Call it learning to live in the world as it is, not as our leaders fantasize it. Call it minding our own business better, and becoming clearer about what that business is, and isn't. Call it a prescription for survival—for ourselves, at least, though perhaps for others, too—for another generation, just one generation at a time.

And if we need more rhetorical support, let it be from our proud and sensible native tradition. It was John Quincy Adams, as Secretary of State (an ardent continental expansionist, incidentally, one of the architects of the present American territorial state) who said, on the Fourth of July, 1821, speaking against intervention to help the Greeks throw off Turkish rule:

> America . . . goes not abroad in search of monsters to destroy. She is the well-wisher to the freedom and independence of all. She is the champion and vindicator only of her own.

As President Carter looks out over the world, he sees "turmoil, strife and change." There's nothing wrong with his eyesight, but there is something wrong with his vision. For he assumes (and this is the heart of interventionism) that "the state of our union depends on the state of the world." In a way, of course, that proposition is a truism. But with the world increasingly out of our control, it is time we made it less true.

Earl C. Ravenal
Washington, D.C.
April 1980

Notes

1.   Able exponents of this position have been Richard Barnet in the *Washington Post* on January 20, 1980 and the *New York Times* Op-Ed page on March 7, 1980, and Arthur Cox in *Newsday* on January 6, 1980.

2.   This one from a press conference on the Carter Doctrine by John J. Gilligan and Paul C. Warnke, as officers of "New Directions," reported in the *Washington Post*, February 20, 1980.

Contents

PART I

INTRODUCTION

CHAPTER 1

Collective Amnesia
or Perpetual Debate?

No comment on history is more frequently or sententiously quoted than that of George Santayana: "Those who cannot remember the past are condemned to repeat it." But how does a nation learn from its own experience?

The crucial question for American foreign policy is how we understand and absorb the failures of the past two decades. Of course, the lessons of Vietnam are a large piece of this problem, but they are not the whole of it. Vietnam is the paradigm, the symbol—and the epitaph—of a generation of expansive foreign policy making and global adventure. But this is not a book about Vietnam. It does not describe the decision making that led to Vietnam or to its fall. It does not make apologies or apportion blame. It is not another set of prescriptions for fighting past wars over again, for doing better next time—whatever "better" and "next time" might mean.

This is a book about how a nation learns from its foreign
policy failures:

It tells what Americans think they have learned from
the past two decades, what they have failed to
learn, and why this matters.

It is an analysis and a summing up of the kinds of
lessons America has been drawing from its experience, and where these lessons go astray or fall short.

Beyond that, it is an introspection—a theoretical excursion—into the way we derive conclusions from
history and apply them to current problems of
foreign policy choice.

Finally, it is a prescription: It asks the perennially
valid and pertinent question: "What is to be done?"
What must be changed, if this country is to avoid
future experiences as burdensome and destructive
as those of the past two decades?

Do we need such an exercise? Why now? Is it too soon?
Or too late? Americans seem to have tired of lessons of
Vietnam. Retrospections of that war started almost before
the events had occurred—certainly long before they were
finished. Perversely, the result is that Americans have tried,
not to learn, but to put the whole era of Vietnam out of
mind, prematurely, before they could draw the appropriate
and effective conclusions. It has been a remarkable case of
collective amnesia.

Of course, part of this forgetfulness is the erosion of time.
The protest songs are echoes now; the legions of demon-
strators are scattered. Most have made their peace with
"the system." Even graduate students in international relations don't remember the problems or identify with the
struggles, and they are eager now to take their policy directions and their career rewards from elders who have a stake
in their own interpretation of America's motives. Neither of
the major political parties has much use for retrospection or
analysis; they are busy setting the conditions for the next
foreign encounter, which will be no better understood. Even

the liberals think they have recovered the ability to distinguish, in the future, between the good wars and the bad ones. Others simply think they have discovered the means to do better. Those who would draw out and amplify the lessons of the recent past are accused of overgeneralizing. The significance of the events of the past two decades is diminished, obscured, repressed.

Perhaps the reason for this amnesia is that Vietnam proved some things that America does not want to admit, some things that it can't reconcile with notions about foreign policy that it is not ready to give up.

It has been said that critics, in the aftermath of any traumatic situation, are likely to be as wrong as those who involved us in it in the first place. Thus, it is said, those who remembered Munich got us into Vietnam. The implication is that the critics of Vietnam will keep us from wielding responsible power in a timely and sufficient way in some future case. By this reasoning, we could have expected an isolationist reaction to Vietnam, something approximating the protracted reaction to the First World War that culminated in the "Munich" syndrome: the twin evils of appeasement and unpreparedness that fanned the ambitions of aggressors at the same time as they almost precluded us from stopping them.

If that is so, the interesting question is, Why are we *not* having our isolationist reaction to Vietnam? Why, instead, have we had an orgy of displaced belligerence—the Mayaguez response, the abortive involvement in Angola, the political intransigence over Panama, the symbolically increased defense budget, the attack on detente, and the debate about the removal of troops from Korea—each in its way a belated surrogate for the unsatisfactorily resolved conflict in Vietnam? The American people, and to some extent the Congress, seem to be fed up with being pushed around by anyone—Russians, third world revolutionaries, terrorists, even recalcitrant allies.

Even more remarkable has been the reaction of our foreign policy elites, both in and out of government—many of them first as critics, out of office, and now as the foreign policy making apparatus. Their reaction has been a campaign, almost a conspiracy of deliberate negligence, to have America *un*learn the lessons of the past two decades— that is, to dissociate the signals of our recent past from the exercise of future foreign policy making.

McGeorge Bundy, for example, has said: ". . . there is at least a great lesson about Vietnam which deserves to be learned and understood by all of us just as soon as possible: it is that the case of Vietnam is unique. It does not make sense to set as a central objective the redesign of our foreign policy so as to avoid 'another Vietnam.'"[1] The purpose of such commentators is to define Vietnam exclusively, to confine its lessons in a narrow specificity, to preserve our ability and will to intervene again in other contexts.[2] These are honorable public servants and intelligent men, who are dedicated to the national interest as they understand it. Precisely because they explain the failures of the past two decades in ways that maintain the integrity of their habitual positions, it is important to examine their critiques. For skewed explanations, false lessons, and comfortable myths are the nemesis of correct future policy—not just toward Asia but toward every region of the world.

Though the various critiques of Vietnam diverge, on one point there will probably remain a coalescence of opinion: that the United States should avoid another encounter conducted as disadvantageously and indecisively and with as much injury to our own society and polity. In fact, everyone says "Never again." But "never again" means several different things. America has not learned the same lesson; and different lessons lead to different future responses and different present dispositions. So one of the tasks of this book is to sort out these divergent critiques, compare and analyze them, and draw out their implications.

We can distinguish five meanings of "never again"—five types of lessons for the future of American foreign policy.[3]

The first four are most prevalent:

1. The instrumental (the establishment's response): We can do better, in various ways, "next time." We should prepare to do so; all we need is better tools—more effective weapons, more decisive tactics, bolder diplomacy.

2. The proportional (the liberal critique): Yes, we made mistakes, but they can be explained away as special cases. The fault was not American intervention, but our persistence in the face of disproportionate costs and our failure to recognize the unique liabilities of the situation. We should pursue selective intervention in the future and retain the flexibility to get out if it is not going well.

3. The consequential (the economic argument): What was wrong was the inefficiency, the distortion of priorities. We should conserve resources, redesign defense programs, transfer expenditures to domestic sectors.

4. The fundamental (the moral and institutional case): We can blame the "crimes" of successive administrations and the inherent nature of the American system. Moral norms should constrain our conduct absolutely, regardless of considerations of national interest; but political, social, and economic institutions will have to change before we can expect a constructive foreign policy.

These divergent critiques are interesting as phenomena. They represent the compass points of the debate about future American foreign policy. But, just as in the parable about the blind men and the elephant, they are peculiar to the situation of the observer; at best they are partially valid and thus misleading in their projected remedies.

There is a fifth critique—one that I think is more accurate and constructive:

5. The strategic (the ultimate strategic lessons): America must make a large-scale strategic adjust-

ment, more complete than we have seen, more
pervasive than is yet realized. We must adjust
our entire foreign policy orientation to the evolving constraints of the international system and
our own domestic system.

This is the kind of lesson that, in its structural depth and
appropriate generality, ought to be drawn from the American experience of the past several decades, epitomized by
Vietnam. The strategic critique differs from the others in
its analysis, conclusions, and prescriptions for the future
of American foreign policy. It takes issue with the others,
and it encompasses and transcends them. Above all, it leads
to a different, and more far-reaching, set of remedies. (Ultimately, analysis is understood and judged by the remedies
that logically flow from it.)

The strategic critique represents a kind of "radical realism" about the way things are and the accommodations
we will have to make. It implies broad changes in the way
we look at "threats" and conceive of "national security."
It also implies a restricted definition of our security perimeter
and the tangible requisites of security. Such a restricted
definition, in turn, leads to a severely reduced force structure. But a revised force structure in itself is not a strategic
lesson; it is merely an instrumental adjustment. The Nixon
Doctrine tended toward a lower conventional force structure; but, since it reaffirmed all of our commitments, it was
only a pseudo-strategic shift. It changed the modalities,
or even prejudiced the success, of interventions; but it
made them no less likely.

True strategic lessons differ from merely instrumental
lessons. Strategic lessons go to the heart of policy choice.
They entail a reorientation of our strategic presumptions
so pervasive that our likely response to future challenges—
as well as to those present instrumentalities, such as alliances and commitments, that obligate or dispose us to
future interventions—would be quite different. In short, the
strategic critique would change our propensity to intervene.[4]

Table 1:

Explanatory models or critiques of Vietnam experience

Model, Critique	Target	Remedy
Instrumental	Restricted methods of warfare, wrong tactics, weapons systems undeveloped or developed too late.	Better tools, sharper and more decisive tactics and doctrines, including appropriate diplomacy (Nixon Doctrine).
Proportional	Faulty intelligence, "mistakes," lack of proportion because of incorrect analysis of nature of adversary and his stakes.	More discriminating intelligence, proportionality of means to ends, ability to "extricate" at point where costs overtake interests.
Consequential	Military-industrial complex, bad trade-offs, wrong priorities.	More efficient outputs on foreign policy side, reordered priorities, attempt to get guns *and* butter, allocation of "peace dividend" to domestic use.
Fundamental	Immorality, "crimes" (especially of presidents), "the system" (economic-institutional) and its objective needs.	Morality in executive branch, dismantling of presidential powers, social revolution, fundamental change in institutions.
Strategic	Basic presumptions about source and nature of challenges and "threats," and about political mandate and "necessity" to respond.	Change in basic strategic presumptions, adjustment to constraints of domestic and international system.

Theory and Practice

The irresolution of the foreign policy debate indicates that there is something not entirely simple about learning from the past. In the case of Vietnam, if the lessons were obvious, they would have been settled long ago, with much greater economy of words and with a good deal less heat. In fact, there are some elusive and disputed questions about the application of history to present foreign policy choice. The questions are theoretical as well as practical, and they are overlapping and interlocked.[5]

First, what constitutes a "lesson"? And what does it mean to say that a *system* has "learned"? I will derive some "lessons about lessons"—criteria for a nation's actually learning from its foreign policy experience.

Then, a distinction must be made between the structure of choice and the policy process. The structure of choice is the array of alternatives and how they are evaluated. The policy process is the thrust of the system toward realizing its complex goals while conforming to multiple constraints, including its institutions and values.

The question of how the policy process works has great practical significance. If lessons were only a matter of a few prescriptions—what certain groups would like to do, perhaps for improving the effectiveness of our forces, or tailoring the cases of intervention, or trimming defense spending, or practicing a more restrictive morality—then they could be exercises in subjective opinion or sheer preference. But lessons also consist of the actual adjustments a system makes to its experience. Vietnam, for example, illustrated as well as influenced the constraints that will affect American foreign policy in the future: the attitudes of the American people, of certain key groups, and of the national leadership; and also the international environment in which these attitudes will be expressed. These actual empirical factors determine the adaptation of the nation's security structures, the metamorphosis of the civil-military relationship, and the evolution of foreign policy. These are part of the policy process. In order to understand them, we need a model of how the policy process works.[6]

A strategic critique must also take into account the structure of choice—that is, how we characterize situations (threats, challenges) and construe alternative responses, and distill a sense of the necessity of national action. The necessity of national action is contingent, of course, on the occurrence of certain events in the environment; but the sense of necessity itself is conditioned, long before those events occur, by more fundamental factors that are deeply imbedded in the policy-making system.

This raises the question of where in the structure of choice and in the policy process changes must be made if they are to be effective and durable—that is, if they are to have a reliable effect on the propensity of the system to intervene in future situations. To have an effect on strategic decisions, the changes must be in the basic presumptions about threats and interests and about the mandate of the political system to respond to them in certain ways. These presumptions are deep cognitive factors, or mind-sets, that influence and underlie our perceptions (though they are not the perceptions themselves).

There is also a question about the definition of *policy*. Policy is the most used, and also the most abused, notion in the bureaucratic lexicon. In most statements, policy is construed as a set of predilections, a codification of right thoughts and good intentions. Actually, policy is more elusive and complex. It can be defined more accurately and usefully as the predictions that a system is constantly making about its own likely future conduct in some state of affairs. The contingent-predictive and the pure-prescriptive aspects of policy are closely related. In fact, as we shall see, strategic lessons for American foreign policy stem from some large-scale predictions about the future of the international system and the American domestic system.

A closely related point concerns sorting out the elements of choice and necessity in decision making. Many analysts talk as if foreign policy decision making were purely voluntary—concerned with predilections and intentions. Many policy prescriptions simply identify desirable goals and the most effective implementing moves, unconstrained by limits, costs, or trade-offs. I call this simplistic procedure *requisite analysis*.

Other analysts subscribe to a doctrine of almost pure necessity. The fundamentalists, for example, typically espouse a kind of economic determinism. Others derive political action from the rigid compulsions of individual personality. What is missing from the first kind of policy analysis, voluntarism and requisite analysis, is the notion of necessity, though it is only conditional necessity ("if we want to do certain things, then our choice is limited to certain acceptable alternatives"). What is missing from the second kind of policy analysis, determinism and compulsion, is the notion of choice, though it is structured and constrained choice.

This is a theoretical, or methodological, problem. But it also has practical implications. The notion that our policy consists of our intention and our will is based implicitly on the persistent illusion that America controls the international system and, concomitantly, our own domestic system. But increasingly, neither of those systems is responsive to the pure preferences, the first choices, of our decision-making elites. The American Century is over. The era of American dominance and control, heralded by Henry Luce and established in the wake of the Second World War, lasted only twenty-five years. Of course, everyone knows it is over. But our policy makers and policy analysts have not absorbed the message, and have not begun to adjust to its implications and consequences. They still want to do the same things in the world, but more cheaply, more palatably. They are still striving to reconcile control with the increasingly arduous and tricky circumstances in which that control is to be exercised.

They have not even developed a language appropriate to the situation we are in. They still talk about "national interests" when no one knows any longer what an "interest" is. Not only the rhetoric but the methodology is obsolete. The typical White House study or State Department tract, that passes for policy analysis, begins with a statement of American interests and proceeds in a stately sequence—a minuet—to the challenges to, or obstacles to, the fulfillment of those interests, then to the changes we must accomplish in order to defeat the challenges or make up the gap, and finally to the implementing moves necessary to bring about those changes.

But what sense does it make to construct a wish-list of

national interests if we know that we don't want to bear the costs and suffer the consequences of attaining them? For this is what has been changing—the constraints, the trade-offs—what we can and can't do in the world, what we must pay to get what we want.

All this should lead to a sense of the limits of foreign policy in a world that is largely given—that is, not of our own individual making or determination. We need a better sense of constraints: those that arise from our international environment and those that arise from the conditions of our own domestic system (our society and our constitution).

Ignoring these constraints—particularly the domestic ones—has become fashionable again among statesmen and political aspirants and their foreign policy advisors, in a sort of backlash to Vietnam. Those who would stress the constraints on intervention and control are castigated as "isolationists" and dismissed as defeatists. A new consensus has formed—indeed, it has congealed—and has come to dominate foreign policy making in the post-Vietnam era, including the foreign policy-making of the Carter administration. But it is a consensus only of foreign policy elites. Moreover, it is a composition of contradictions and is correspondingly fragile.[7] The essence of the strategic critique is that this superficial consensus doesn't matter. Constraints are existential and objective; they are features of the foreign policy landscape. They constitute powerful—though contingent—inhibitions on the projection of our foreign policy, and our policy-making elites will have to cope with them, some day.

Closely related to this question of necessity is how we characterize the decisions of the past. Many analysts, for example, call the decisions to intervene and escalate in Vietnam "mistakes." It is closer to the mark to consider those decisions as choices, even if there were elements of error. This is not a scholastic or abstract point. It bears on the predictions we make about intervention in future situations.

Vietnam was indeed a choice, not a mistake. The fact that it was a disaster does not mean that it was a mistake, and it is important to see why this is so. In the structure of choice at the time, not to intervene was seen to lead to even worse consequences. And in the policy process of the time, intervention was the indicated result—even a conditional necessity—because our government could not have withstood the political costs of default. I do not mean absolute necessity—only that our decision-making system would have done the same things again even if it had known how they would turn out, because the feared consequences of the opposite course were seen as still worse. A *mistake*, by contrast, is a decision that an actor would not repeat if he knew how it would turn out.

No additional or superior information or intelligence would have altered the actions that were taken by the United States. Therefore, more information is not a sufficient condition (and is probably not even a necessary condition) for doing better in the future. What we need is not more information but more constructive decision rules for future conduct.

This is not the usual judgment on intervention and escalation in Vietnam. The important corollary of this judgment is that our system will do the same thing again, in similar—or even dissimilar but structurally analogous—situations, unless there is a change at the level where such a change would be effective and reliable. That implies a change in our strategic presumptions about the nature of national security in an uncertain and constrained world. That is the essence of the strategic critique of the foreign policy decisions of the past, and it is the link between the understanding of the past and the prescription of policy for the future.

If an analysis is not correct—that is, if it does not locate the source of national action—then it will not indicate the requisite change in our foreign policy orientations. Thus, we should not seek to know what mistakes we made, but why our system made the choices it did. There is no reason to believe that the choices in the future will lie between some "correct" course—favorable in its consequences and without cost and risk—and some "mistaken" course. Rather, the choices will be between losses of one kind or another. Far from optimizing outcomes, we will be concerned to avoid fundamental or irreversible damage. Therefore, we will have to make a wide and general adjustment to our situation in the world. That, again, is the essence of the strategic critique.

What We Expect from Our Foreign Policy

If anything must change, it is our expectations of foreign policy. We must reverse the persistent attitude of American control that has been conditioned into our foreign policy reflexes for the past thirty years. We must recover a sense of the limits of foreign policy in a world that is no longer malleable. Foreign policy must be seen not as a lance but as a shield. It is not a vehicle for propagating our values or a pretext for projecting our fantasies, but a set of minimum conditions for preserving our vital internal processes. Occasionally, but rarely, we may face a situation in which our highest honor is embodied in the struggle of another people in the world. But our primary business is to operate our unique political system, enjoy and enhance our economic activities, and repair and perfect our society. The justification for foreign commitments and defense expenditures is to protect those essential purposes. Therefore, attaining "essential equivalence" of means of destruction with some designated adversary is a distraction and an irrelevance; and it is meaningless to have "more security" than we need. We can spend more, but security is finite: Either we are safe or we are not.

The past thirty years have been a unique period in our history and in the evolution of the international system. The historical conditions in which attitudes of American control were formed have come to an end. Constraints on intervention have multiplied. Externally, the superpowers

substantially neutralize each other. Regional contenders
assert themselves. Revolutionary movements acquire intrinsic strength and access to outside support. Nationalisms
of the left and the right defy gunboat diplomacy and dominate resources. Internally, the impediments to effective
foreign policy have been evident and pervasive. There is
now a nexus of interacting factors: the gains of intervention are predictably smaller; the costs are foreseeably
greater; public support is less reliable; our perseverance
is less certain; outcomes, even if favorable, are temporary.

These are general phenomena, not peculiar to Vietnam.
Conversely, Vietnam, far from being an aberrant case,
nonreplicable and therefore dispensable, is significant as
an indication of the passing of the conditions that formerly
enabled and facilitated American intervention. For these
reasons, the strategic critique is not just another lesson,
and a belated one at that; it is an early warning of the need
for a foreign policy appropriate to our new circumstances.
We must move from exercises of control to exercises of
adjustment, from projecting our national values to pro-
tecting them.

Of course, these are not yet acceptable propositions in
the world of "responsible" foreign policy discussion. Attitudes of American control—though they are increasingly
irrelevant to the new shape of the world and the new domestic conditions—persist. Elites are still committed to policies and rationales—whether instrumentalist, proportionalist,
or consequentialist—that could lead merely to cheaper and
more "decisive" modes of intervention. And analysts are
still proposing techniques and organizational forms—whether
unilateral or collective (condominium, universal organizations, alliances, or the balance of power)—that would perpetuate American control. Attitudes of conflict management
and manipulation prevail. Attitudes of nonintervention and
conflict avoidance are not yet fashionable.

In fact, since the Vietnam war, the hawks have regained
much of their ground and have reasserted their custody

of the national interest and the symbols of patriotism. In this respect, the real losers of the Vietnam war have been the humanitarian left, who tried to introduce a new set of values, a new calculus, into American foreign policy; their defeat is a profound and not yet recognized loss to the nation.[8] Congress jumps clear of having its skirts muddied by the charge of isolationism; it concedes the substance of larger defense budget requests of successive administrations, while recording pro forma objections and asserting procedural prerogatives. Strategic analysts who want to be taken seriously burnish their credibility again with ominous talk about southern Africa, the Horn of Africa, the Indian Ocean, and the Persian Gulf, and the need for a militant American response.

All this demonstrates that what we have unlearned or mislearned from the experience of the past several decades might be more important than the experience itself. Despite the surfeit of retrospection, we have tried to suppress, without ever really absorbing, the lessons of our recent history. We are in danger of distorting our past and misapplying it to our future.

But also, whether or not we like it or even admit it, we will spend many more years digesting and debating the experience of Vietnam. This debate will take the form of more general propositions about America's role in the world. In that sense, the experience of Vietnam has become part of the perpetual debate about the premises of American foreign policy.

PART II

LESSONS

CHAPTER 2

Lessons about Lessons:
Cat on a Hot Coal Stove

Is America's reading of the lessons of Vietnam so pre-emptive that the country has lost its capacity and will to wage an active, responsible foreign policy? Many observers fear this. Alastair Buchan cautioned:

> America's mistake in Vietnam does not invalidate the vital principle that countries invaded by their neighbours should be assured of international help. . . . Successive American Presidents thought that in Vietnam they were upholding the basic principle of world order. The United States has now withdrawn from the disastrous consequences of making a political misjudgment. It would be an even greater disaster if the US were now to conclude that the principle itself was foolish.[1]

Such observers see America acting like Mark Twain's legendary cat. Twain said: "We should be careful to get out of an experience only the wisdom that is in it—and stop there; lest we be like the cat that sits down on a hot stove lid. She will never sit down on a hot stove lid again—and that is well; but also she will never sit down on a cold one."[2] Most commentators have grasped this point, and many have cited Twain's cat approvingly. Lincoln P. Bloomfield says:

> We need to learn our lessons from the years of scourge, but also to bear in mind Mark Twain's injunction not to get out of an experience more than there is in it ("A cat . . .").[3]

Curiously, Henry Kissinger was impressed by the same example, but he used it to argue for accurately identifying the present case, rather than for denying the scope of the historical analogue:

> The lessons of historical experience . . . are contingent. They teach the consequences of certain actions, but they cannot force a recognition of comparable situations. An individual may have experienced that a hot stove burns but, when confronted with a metallic object of a certain size, he must decide from case to case whether it is in fact a stove before his knowledge will prove useful.[4]

In their fascination with the cat and the stove, these commentators beg the critical questions in applying Twain's parable to national policy decisions, particularly armed interventions: (1) How do you know a stove is not hot until you sit on it, at which point it is too late? (2) Why do you want or need to sit on any stove, hot or cold? In fact, we learn by categories; more important, we act according to categories. The appropriate questions about categories are not whether to respect them at all, but (a) how fine it is intelligible to cut them, and (b) how fine it is prudent to cut them.

In any case, the fear that America will overgeneralize from Vietnam is misplaced. Rather, most of the conclusions drawn from that experience have been so qualified, so particularized, that they amount to the unexceptionable resolution that we should not fight Vietnam over again. For example, Samuel P. Huntington admonishes:

> We have all along been familiar with Santayana's warning that if we do not remember the past we shall be condemned to repeat it. In the debates over Vietnam, a counter-warning has frequently been voiced . . . that if we remember the past we are condemned to misread it. . . . It is conceivable that our policy-makers may best meet future crises and dilemmas if they simply blot out of their mind any recollection of this one. The right lesson, in short, may be the unlesson. . . . Every historical event or confluence of events obviously is unique.[5]

Francis E. Rourke asserts:

> Critics of the war as well as its defenders often tended to stake out more extravagant positions on the meaning of Vietnam than were justified by the rather unique circumstances of that conflict.[6]

More recently, warning against the (mis-)application of Vietnam to the Middle East, the *New Republic* opined:

> It is important to remind ourselves that the case against the Vietnam war was concrete and specific. Indeed its opponents insisted on its particularity. . . . The war . . . was wrong for *reasons*, and for similar reasons, we must be prepared to oppose similar wars. But not necessarily all wars or all use (or threats) of force. It would be foolish to cling to an arbitrarily consistent policy that disregards all possible cases. . . . [A]n absolute commitment to abjure force, whatever the provocation, is as dangerous as a promiscuous commitment to fight one little war after another.[7]

And now, referring to an American withdrawal from Korea, Donald S. Zagoria enthusiastically cites James C. Thomson's arch conclusion:

> The only lesson we should learn from Vietnam, he said, is never again to fight a nationalist movement

dominated by Communists in a former French col-
ony.[8]

Of course, these people can score easy points by remind-
ing us of circumstantial differences and superficial dis-
similarities. The irony is that so many of them are historians,
of one sort or another. For, in these essays in historical
particularism, or literalism, they invite us to curtail the
exercise of identification and comparison to the point where
our powers of recognition and analogy would atrophy entirely. In asking that we be careful with history, they would
deny history.

Why is history interesting at all? And what does *interesting* even mean? At stake is not just the use of history but
also its meaning and even its existence. Without generaliza-
tion and extrapolation, our experience disintegrates beyond
intelligible recovery, let alone useful application. The very
existence of history depends on the ability to reconstruct
and appropriate our experience by general categories. Moreover, when one attacks the legitimacy of generalizing from
experience, one is questioning nothing less than whether we
can predicate anything (any quality or characteristic) of a
generality (a genus, a class, a category, a type), and thus,
conversely, whether we can extrapolate (draw wider conclusions) from any single instance that we recognize as
belonging to that class—in short, whether we can learn anything or predict anything. So we are in danger of losing
not only our sense of history but also our handle on reality.[9]

It is no less ironic that some of those who were most
articulate in condemning Vietnam have been most reluctant
to draw sufficiently general conclusions from that experience. A cardinal example is former Under Secretary of
State George Ball. Ball's analysis embodies all three elements of the classic "proportional" critique:[10] (1) our conduct
was disproportional to the importance of our interest; (2)
Vietnam was unique; and (3) our intervention was a mistake. From a restricted characterization of Vietnam comes
a restricted judgment of its lessons. "The first and most

fundamental error" is the misperception of "the character of the conflict":

> . . . unlike Korea, the struggle in Vietnam was no mere power thrust by Communists lusting to take over the South, but rather the continuance of a revolution already in progress for three decades to drive out the white man and unite Vietnam—and ultimately all Indochina—under Communist control.

From this characterization, Ball derives his first lesson:

> Before we engage our military power in a foreign land we should make quite certain that we comprehend the nature of the struggle and the play of forces it represents.

Then, asking the question: "Why did our military effort flounder so long and inconclusively?" Ball reasons toward a second lesson:

> . . . we failed not from military ineptitude but because there was no adequate indigenous political base on which our power could be emplaced. And that provides another lesson we must learn if we are to avoid the same mistake a second time.

Summing up his lessons (along somewhat different dimensions), Ball arrives at what sounds like a severe restriction on intervention, but is actually doubly qualified:

> The obvious lesson from all this is that America must never again commit its power and authority [1] in defense of a country of only marginal strategic interest [2] when that country lacks a broadly based government, or the will to create one. [Numbers added.]

It should not escape notice that this double condition (no strategic importance and no political viability) considerably narrows the stricture against future intervention. This is not just a debating point but is the heart of the matter. It allows intervention whenever strategic interests alone seem compelling (and it might also allow intervention to support a popular—or even potentially popular—government, even if it is strategically marginal). In fact, Ball does not

leave us to speculate about his own position in this matter.
He is interested in restricting the lessons of Vietnam because he wants to carve out a wide area for future intervention:

> If one believes as I do, that in spite of the problems
> it poses for a democracy, the United States may find
> it necessary from time to time to use limited force
> in certain strategic areas where important security
> interests are directly threatened and where limited
> intervention would offer the prospects of effective
> deterrence—as, for example, in some parts of the
> Middle East or Latin America. . . .

Maybe so. But we have to remember that, at the beginning,
Vietnam also seemed to be a case of strategic necessity.

What is not so "obvious" from Ball's criteria is how Vietnam should have been classified at various points: whether
it was a mistake from the start; whether it became a mistake
through fruitless escalation matched at all stages by the
adversary; whether it became a mistake after the diplomatic
isolation of Hanoi through the geopolitics of Nixon and
Kissinger in Peking and Moscow; or whether it became a
mistake only in retrospect, because, having put some history between us and the episode, we could then afford the
conclusion that it did not matter as much as we once thought
it did. These questions must be sorted out, if the "mistake"
of Vietnam is to be avoided in the future—or rather, if the
choice of another Vietnam is to be declined in the future.
These questions can be sorted out only by another view of
the nature of the war and a more ample conception of its
lessons.

It is worth taking some time to analyze the notion of
lessons, to draw some conclusions about these intellectual
products of history—in short, to learn some lessons about
lessons. If lessons are to be useful and reliable, if they are
not to be simply discrete judgments about a single unrepli-
cable past event or series of events, they must meet certain
requirements.

First, they must be *projective*—forward-looking, referring to the future. (In this respect they differ from judgments, which are only retrospective.) This is so whether they are prescriptive, relating to what we ought to do, or predictive, relating to what we probably will do under certain circumstances.

Second, lessons must be *general*, or, more accurately, generic. They must be about something larger than the particular case that gave rise to them. More graphically, they must lie along some intelligible dimension of action— such a dimension as intervention/nonintervention or morality/amoralism. An event (such as Vietnam) is an instance of some more general principle; thus, its lessons should have a wider scope of application.

Third, lessons must be *appropriate* to the activity that gave rise to them. In this case, it is not enough to draw moral lessons or to make points about the impact of personality on politics. The lessons must be strategic, in two senses: they must apply to defense preparations, security commitments, intervention, and war; and they must become part of the structure and process of strategic choice. Of course, strategic choice itself is complicated, or enhanced, by its inclusion of moral choice—that is, it must be decided whether the tangible value to be defended is worth the sacrifice of moral values, or, vice versa, whether the defense of certain moral values (such as a type of political system, the honor of a nation's commitments, the protection of a threatened population) is worth the risk or sacrifice of certain tangible values. The ultimate strategic question is how much we care about certain objects of policy. Historical lessons must bear upon these questions of strategic choice and national values.

Fourth, lessons are not lessons unless they are *learned*. This is far from an obvious proposition (except perhaps to a Berkeleian empiricist, to whom nothing exists until it is perceived and comprehended). The learning of a collective—a whole and complex entity such as a nation-state—

is different from the learning of an individual or a narrow decision-making group. Lessons must be internalized in some enduring, objective, consistent, and therefore predictable way. They may be institutionalized, embodied in new or revised procedures, preparations, dispositions; or they may take the form of new constraints or conditions that are added to the policy process. In that case, the lessons may consist of these constraints themselves, as we shall see when we consider how the American policy-making system has actually adapted to the experience of Vietnam. Thus, learning a lesson means impressing upon the structure and process of policy choice a set of decision rules ("if-then" propositions), often in concrete form, that will dispose the system to respond in certain ways—presumably better than before—to future contingencies.

If we look at lessons in this rather complex and structured way, it is apparent that the lessons of Vietnam, even several years after the experience, are far from settled. There are several reasons for this. One is that the coalition—or coalescence—of various forces that brought pressures on our government to move to a quicker termination of the war— whether by negotiation, coercive escalation, or unilateral withdrawal—was not a true consensus. It was a patchwork of motives, perceptions, and values. It included disgust that "effective" or "decisive" extensions and types of warfare had been ruled out; the feeling that the level and scope of war had gone beyond the importance of the American interests involved; doubt that these interests had even justified intervention in the first place; alarm at the distortion of priorities and the diversion of scarce or otherwise-needed resources; dismay at the immorality of the prosecution of the war, the occasional atrocities and excesses, and the corruption and repressive behavior of our allies; the resentment of the legislative branch at the extension and abuse of executive war-making power; the partisan desire to embarrass successive administrations; and the political accommodation of certain constituencies, particularly younger voters.

The pressures of this diverse anti-Vietnam coalition foreclosed certain options to our government and forced an inconclusive end to the American phase of the war, in the Paris accords of January 1973. But this temporary and fragile coalition was soon fractured. Consequently, its impact on future strategic choices is not clear. Indeed, the various meanings of "no more Vietnams," in diverse future circumstances, will almost certainly be mutually contradictory.

The second reason for the indeterminacy of the lessons of Vietnam is that, for more than two years after the Paris accords, it was not settled who had "won" the war. Winning or losing are partially a function of the purpose for which a war was fought (and the declarations of several administrations only add to the confusion about that purpose). For one thing, Vietnam was scarcely ever conceived as a war to be won or lost in the classic sense (as were the First and Second World Wars). For another, the Vietnam war endured so long that several sets of rationales were shot out from under the same ongoing action.

In the beginning, our intervention may have been a last attempt to implement collective security. Some of the rhetoric of Secretary of State Dean Rusk suggests that Vietnam was, in his estimation and that of other influential policy makers, the limiting case of the same principle of collective security that had inspired our earlier intervention in Korea. If this was its purpose, Vietnam was almost a *reductio ad absurdum*. "Collective" security was thinly exercised essentially by one nation, the United States (despite the presence of a few other flags such as South Korea—which, however, had to be richly induced to join in the war[11]). The rationale of collective security required the repulse of aggression and the exemplary punishment of the aggressor. By these standards, Vietnam was scarcely a victory.

In its middle phase, the Vietnam war evolved so that the perceived and intended adversary was China, supposedly operating through the proxies of North Vietnam and the

Vietcong. By the rules of bipolar confrontation, victory would have required the clear defeat of the adversary, at least in the limited theater of challenge. In this sense also, the encounter was no success.

In its final phase, with the accession of Nixon and Kissinger, the war became something else: an exercise in the balance of power. Victory in such circumstances requires less than in the previous ones. Even a tenuous stalemate, an equilbrium based on continuing conflict, could be counted as success. In a balance of power policy, the entire engagement may be indefinite, but discrete actions should be decisive. They must simply create a reputation for response, provide an object lesson to any potential adversary that we will contest—not necessarily succeed in repelling—attempts to change guaranteed frontiers, seize essential resources, deny strategic access, or achieve powerful psychological momentum (the new version of the "dominoes"). Thus, in Nixon and Kissinger's reading of Vietnam, the real adversary became, once again, a major communist power, the Soviet Union. The Soviets were the "real" adversary in a different sense, however; it was not simply because they were the bankers of the large conventional North Vietnamese offensive of April 1973. Rather, it was because the Soviets were the only significant "objective" opponents— either the inevitable pupils of a decisive American response or the inescapable beneficiaries of a local failure on our part. (That same logic, according to the Ford-Kissinger administration, pertained in Angola.) By frustrating direct challengers and implicit beneficiaries alike, we teach them the rules of the new international political-military game. In this sense—in contesting the challenge, escalating the war, gaining a stalemate for a time—the United States arguably achieved some degree of success in Vietnam. (Undoubtedly, Kissinger will reflect this rationale in his memoirs, as he did in his policies and actions.)

But even this partial success was blurred by America's

final default in the end game of spring 1975. Thus, the shifting rationales, and the various interpretations of partial success and final failure, confuse the lessons that might be drawn from this experience.

Another difficulty in drawing lessons from Vietnam is that, in evaluating the consequences of one course of action, one is implicitly comparing them with the consequences of the courses not taken—the "might have beens," in President Eisenhower's phrase. I don't agree with Eisenhower's judgment ". . . speculation as to 'might have beens' is—as always—scarcely more than an exercise in futility";[12] but comparing intervention and abstention does pose a peculiar problem: there is an asymmetry in the tests that are typically applied. Intervention is later condemned if the cumulative costs are excessive; whatever undesirable consequences were prevented are taken for granted. On the other hand, abstention or default is later condemned if aggression against a friendly state or a valuable strategic position succeeds or results in the critical enhancement of the position or power of a hostile state; then the considerable costs that might have been spared are taken for granted. In other words, intervention is judged by its costs, non-intervention by its consequences. It is hard enough to specify the hypothetical consequences of our never having intervened in Southeast Asia, let alone to compare them with the known costs of our ten or fifteen year intervention. The lessons of this experience are further complicated and obscured.

All this does not mean that there are no lessons to be learned, or that we can afford to unlearn the ones that are there. Those historians and statesmen who urge us to ignore and unlearn would deny the implications of our national experience precisely because they wish to avoid its consequences. Indeed, they go further and deny even the blank requirement for a decent consistency of national behavior over time and across space because they don't want to be bound in the future by the lessons of the past. In the "case-by-case" treatment of past lessons and present decisions, historical amnesia is joined with policy pointillism. Perhaps the final comment on such irresponsibility of interpretation and deed is the cynical passage in Christopher Marlowe's *The Jew of Malta*:

> Thou hast committed—
> Fornication—but that was in another country;
> And besides, the wench is dead.

CHAPTER 3

Overworking the
Munich Analogy

Exception-mongering—refusing to learn lessons from history—is all too prevalent. Nevertheless, a historical analogy can be carried too far, especially if it is drawn out in the wrong direction. *Munich* is the arch-example. The analogy of *Munich* and the lesson of *appeasement* have been imported into every significant debate about American intervention since the Second World War. Every move away from war and the preparation for war, every suggestion of *detente*, every congressional obstruction of executive action, every proposal of a retrenched or disengaged foreign policy, whether in a region or across the board, has been condemned as appeasement, an invitation or a surrender to aggression.

In particular, there is the question of applying the Munich analogy to Vietnam. Would abstention from Vietnam or a unilateral withdrawal have violated the proper lessons of Munich? Or, on the contrary, did our initial involvement in

Vietnam proceed from our overlearning the lessons of
Munich? There is some truth in the latter charge. Just
note Lyndon Johnson's statement supporting his conception of the dominoes in Southeast Asia: "We learned from
Hitler at Munich that success only feeds the appetite of
aggression. The battle would be renewed in one country
after another country."[1] But, if anything, we had not over-
learned; we had *mis*learned, and *mis*applied.

Later, the critics began to recover their conventional
senses and to cite Munich in the usual, careless way. De-
crying a precipitate American withdrawal from Vietnam,
they urged using our remaining coercive force to obtain
concessions from our adversary. The objective was to have
something to show for all our effort—a fair and durable
peace, a "peace with honor." For example, the appeasement label was applied by the Nixon administration and the
centrist liberal critics alike to candidate McGovern's proposal for complete, unconditional, unilateral withdrawal.
Even columnists such as Joseph Kraft of the *Washington
Post* condemned McGovern for being "prepared to accept
worse terms than the other side is offering."[2] The reaction
of James Reston of the *New York Times* was to insist that
"surely there is something in between the President's policy . . . and McGovern's policy"[3]—presumably because he
did not like the consequences of either (a classic example
of the liberal's unerring choice of the unavailable middle
solution).

More recently, a fiercer spirit of recrimination has taken
hold. Some have applied the Munich critique to the congressional cutoff of funds and the curtailment of executive
latitude that led to the fall of Vietnam in April 1975. Martin
Peretz, editor of the *New Republic*, supported an accusation
that the American peace movement had foreclosed the
chances for a compromise "political settlement" and forced
an abject American defeat: "Much of the American left
has on its record having rooted in Vietnam and Cambodia
for the gangsters of ideology. . . . the American collapse

will read in history as among the ugliest of national crimes."[4]

False analogies between Munich and more recent proposals of disengagement or nonintervention spring not only
(1) from misconceptions of the more recent proposals for
disengagement—whether in Vietnam, Taiwan, Angola, or
Korea—but also (2) from misconceptions of what happened
at Munich and in its aftermath and of what the dimensions
of appeasement are. Confusions following from the lessons
of Munich are not entirely due to false analogies; the mis-
characterization of Munich has contributed its own distortions.

It is possible, by various literary devices, to outline
Munich as a surrender of territory and neglect of defense
and then to assimilate it to later situations, such as the
late-Vietnam withdrawal demands of the doves, the post-
Vietnam calls for a retrenched global posture, and even
the present moves toward detente with the Soviet Union.
A recent attempt to reconstruct the events and postures of
Munich and apply them to our time has been made by
Edward Luttwak.[5] By making striking and ironic juxta-
positions of Churchill's premonitions with the warnings of
such present-day hawks as the Committee on the Present
Danger, Luttwak confers upon the latter, and himself, some
of the same gifts of prophecy that he discerns in Churchill:

> Twenty-seven days later Britain was at war—the un-
> necessary war, as Churchill was later to call it, caused
> by the British and French failure to undertake the
> measures of military preparedness which might have
> deterred the Germans from their aggressive designs
> and which might have led to the eventual overthrow
> of Hitler from within.

To the extent that such articles themselves indicate, and
promote, a growing polarization of the foreign policy debate, we may indeed be living in an era that parallels the
1930s. But there is a flaw of interpretation.

The outbreak of general war in Europe in 1939 might have
been "unnecessary," but the implication that the fault was

simply the British and French policy of nonintervention is neither historically justified nor logically indicated. Rather, the fault might have been too much intervention, at first in active appeasement of Hitler over the Sudetenland and later in overreliance on deterrent threat and bluff (Britain's blank-check commitment to Poland in March 1939). If anything, it was the abrupt and imprudent abandonment of appeasement in the East by Britain and France that brought on the more general European war of September 1939.[6]

It is not the purpose of this brief analysis to argue the merits of appeasement. Quite the contrary. The purpose is to redefine the concept analytically and to distinguish it from nonintervention, with which it has often been confused. Nonintervention and appeasement are at polar odds. The difference can be made apparent by citing two characteristics of a posture of nonintervention: (1) it is indifferent to consequences, not a means of bringing about an improvement in the outcome of the situation, and (2) it is unilateral, not a concerted or interactive strategy. Appeasement differs in both aspects. First, it is interventionist, involved in consequences in a manipulative and actively coercive way. This is particularly true of its most striking historical manifestation. What is characteristic of Munich is that the British and French put great pressure on Czechoslovakia, a friendly power over which they had leverage, to accede to the demands of Hitler, in order to avoid being involved in a war at that time and place that they were ill-equipped and reluctant to wage. They even seized the initiative from Hitler and coerced their ally to make a timely and (they hoped) sufficient concession.[7] Not that the British and French should necessarily have issued a guarantee to President Benes of Czechoslovakia, a warning to Hitler, and a call to the Russians for collective assistance. The point is that both of the choices perceived by Britain and France, appeasement or resistance, were active and interventionist. Simple nonintervention was not within their field of decision.

Second, appeasement is highly interactive, not unilateral. The smaller ally is threatened with abandonment for refusing to make concessions; continuing help is both promised for and predicated on its making concessions. The irony is that the larger ally is then more implicated in a position of less strength, and the smaller ally is more dependent on a less reliable guarantor. (Henry Kissinger's coercive step-by-step diplomacy toward Israel after October 1973 is strongly suggested. The real parallel is President Carter's pressure on Israel to cede the West Bank to some sort of Palestinian control.) It was the multilateral meddling of Britain and France in the dispute between Nazi Germany and Czechoslovakia over the Sudeten Germans that defused Czech resistance and set the stage for Czech capitulation. Indeed, Hitler sought the active involvement of Britain and France precisely in order to escalate the stakes, which might otherwise have remained local and limited. It was necessary for Hitler to involve the Western powers, to use their fear of war to cause them, not to abandon, but to coerce Czechoslovakia. (This too suggests the Middle East situation. In initiating the war of October 1973, the Egyptians and Syrians appear to have had a similar motive. In a rough analogue of Munich, the United States accepted the gambit and played the role of active appeaser, using its leverage to cause Israel to withdraw from forward military positions. In Vietnam, Nixon employed something like reverse appeasement: by diplomacy with Russia and China, by escalating the war, and by mining Haiphong harbor, he sought to induce North Vietnam's supporters to put pressure on Hanoi to come to terms with the United States.)

From this perspective, it is easy to see how misconceived were the charges of appeasement that met McGovern's withdrawal proposal in 1972. Hanoi was attempting to secure U. S. connivance in toppling the Thieu government in Saigon and imposing a communist-dominated coalition. The course of appeasement, combining active intervention with multilateral involvement, would have been to accede to these pressures and coerce our ally in order to gain a cease-fire and allow American extrication. (In fact, the actions taken by Nixon and Kissinger bear some resemblance to this course.) The course of nonintervention and disengagement would have been diametrically opposite: to get out unilaterally and completely, with no coercion of allies or bargains with adversaries. The results would have been different, too. As for allies, we would have been serving notice that it is conceivable that some are not worth supporting, by any calculus of cost or gain. As for adversaries, they might have had reason to fear that they would lose some of their influence in the situation by losing their leverage on the United States.

In sharp distinction from appeasement, a strategy of nonintervention and disengagement is indifferent to the adversary's gain or loss. Not that a nation is unaffected by the situation; rather, it takes a stance of objective indifference toward the differential outcome of the situation. It is this basis of indifference that allows disengagement to be both unconditional and unilateral.

Appeasement, on the other hand, leads typically to two related errors: (1) delivering an ally to bring about a settlement, the mistake of the British and French toward Czechoslovakia at Munich; and (2) then guaranteeing the settlement, or otherwise attempting to stabilize it, as in reestablishing the local balance of power. The trouble is that the balancing process can move in ever wider circles—local, regional, global—creating finally a universal significance and stake in a particular situation. The irony of appeasement is that, in being concerned with outcomes, the appeaser is never really extricated but becomes mortgaged to the new, and less favorable, situation that it has actively helped to establish.

That is the true lesson of Munich.

CHAPTER 4

Was Vietnam a Mistake?

A new myth has emerged—the myth that the Vietnam war was a "mistake." This is the myth of the critical but loyal liberal center—those who earlier supported the main thrust of the American effort in Indochina, dissenting in midstream on points of efficiency or morality. These critics diverge as to how clear and how serious was the mistake, but to all of them it was a matter of error, and the error was not fundamental but circumstantial. The mistake theory appears in two versions.

In the first, it is held that the executive authorities responsible for the crucial decisions to intervene and escalate (that is, Presidents Kennedy and Johnson and their immediate advisors) specifically ignored, at certain critical junctures, the analysis and advice that might have indicated a different course. This would refer to estimates by the intelligence community, particularly the CIA, about the strength and stamina of the enemy; the advice of military experts, such as General Maxwell Taylor in 1962, who

39

warned that only the infusion of a large number of American ground forces would be sufficient to do the job; or the memoranda of Under Secretary of State George W. Ball in 1964 and 1965, who was skeptical of any purely military solution, particularly one sought by bombing.[1] This view derives from inside sources—memos, estimates, private briefs, and debates within government. The thesis is that the advice was so persuasive that it is clear—at least in retrospect—that it should have been accepted.

In the second version, it is held that the prevailing views and shared beliefs of the entire government were generally mistaken about the character of the conflict and the nature of the enemy. In this interpretation, the estimates of the nature of the civil conflict in Vietnam and the capabilities of Communist China turned out to be wrong. A variant of this view is that the war *became* a mistake—at least an objective mistake—as the Sino-Soviet split developed, as the power struggle in China extruded into command positions a faction (Mao, Chou, and at that time Lin) that disfavored active intervention in the Vietnam war, or as the diplomacy of Nixon and Kissinger partially defused China's support for North Vietnam and diplomatically isolated Hanoi.

Both of these versions of the mistake theory are judgments—attempts to indict but also exonerate, in careful mixture, a succession of American governments. They are usually offered as lessons. But the mistake theory begs the essential question that differentiates judgments from lessons: it assumes that, had the true facts that were presented or revealed been believed and accepted, the right conclusions and actions would have followed. Thus, the explanation of our intervention would be: at best, the obscurity of certain facts; at the middling estimate, blindness, self-delusion, wishfulness; and, at the worst, willful negligence and even duplicity in the treatment of these facts and their predictive significance.

This judgment of error ignores the live possibility that, even if the decision makers had appreciated the intelligence and advice to which they were exposed, they would still have acted as they did and set the United States on the course of intervention and escalation in Vietnam. In other words, there were not mistakes, but *choices*: arrays of substantive alternatives and acts of choice—the course that was chosen and the courses that were not chosen and the costs and consequences of each, real or hypothetical. The mistake theory puts the whole matter on the wrong basis. The attribution of error produces only judgments of past performance. True and usable lessons proceed only from the analysis of deliberate choice.

(Neither of these two variants of the mistake theory assert that the president was persuaded by false or overly optimistic reports and prognoses, or that he was isolated or excluded, by misdirected individuals or by the characteristics of the information system, from constructive analysis and advice. The latter explanation tends, rather, to be offered by bureaucratically-inclined analysis.[2] Such bureaucratic analysis concentrates on distorted decision-making processes and the pathological behavior of organizations; it leads characteristically to prescriptions for reforming and restructuring organizations and information systems, and sometimes the incentive patterns that underlie them. The bureaucratic type of analysis and its prescriptions could be considered to belong to the instrumental critique.[3])

A Matter of Choice

The mistake theory can be rejected in various ways, and each way leads to a different set of remedies for American foreign policy. Two prominent critiques that reject the mistake theory of progressive American involvement in Vietnam are those of Leslie H. Gelb and Daniel Ellsberg. Gelb's argument is this:

> Our Presidents and most of those who influenced their decisions did not stumble step by step into Vietnam, unaware of the quagmire. U. S. involvement did not stem from a failure to forsee consequences.

. . . Those who led the United States into Vietnam
did so with their eyes open, knowing why, and be-
lieving they had the will to succeed. The deepening
involvement was not inadvertent, but mainly deduc-
tive. It flowed with sureness from the perceived stakes
and attendant high objectives. . . . Debates revolved
around how to do things better, and whether they
could be done, not whether they were worth doing.
. . . [N]o systematic or serious examination of Vietnam's importance to the United States was ever
undertaken within the government. Endless asser-
tions passed for analysis. . . . Each President was
essentially doing what he thought was minimally
necessary to prevent a Communist victory during his
tenure in office.[4]

Gelb criticizes the narrow instrumentalism that prevailed
within government during the Vietnam escalation. He also
believes, as I do, that "political solutions," such as that
proposed by George Ball,[5] were never really available:
"Most of our leaders and their critics did see that Vietnam
was a quagmire, but did not see that the real stakes—who
shall govern Vietnam—were not negotiable." While Ball con-
tended that the nature of the struggle made negotiation
imperative, Gelb contends that this very feature made
negotiated peace impossible: ". . . the real struggle in Vietnam was not between sovereign states. It was a civil war
for national independence." Furthermore, according to Gelb,
"our Presidents, it seems, recognized that there was no
middle ground."

Thus, Gelb rejects the theses of inadvertence (the "quagmire") and succumbing to bad advice ("the light at the end
of the tunnel"). He also rejects the first mistake theory
specified above: that the president willfully or negligently
rejected good advice. But Gelb does more or less embrace
the second of the above mistake theories: he blames Vietnam on shared beliefs—sincere but wrong—about the nature
and stakes of the conflict. He attributes the "perseverance" of

American presidents (1) to the legacy of their predecessors, the actual moves that had been made in Vietnam, and the stake, however artificial, that these had created; and (2) more important, to "the domino theory, which was at the heart of the matter . . . the widely shared attitude that security was indivisible, that weakness in one place would only invite aggression in others. . . . [T]hey believed in what they were doing on the national security 'merits'."

In alleging a mistake on this higher plane, Gelb adopts a version of the "proportional" critique (the disproportion of means and ends), somewhat tinged with the "consequential" (the diversion of resources): "It is because the price of attaining this goal (. . . to prevent the loss of Vietnam to Communism . . .) has been so dear in lives, trust, dollars, and priorities, and the benefits so intangible, remote, and often implausible, that these leaders and we ourselves are forced to seek new answers and new policies." He identifies the way in which these "new answers" are to be found:

> Paradoxically, the way to get these new answers is not by asking why did the system fail, but why did it work so tragically well. There is, then, only one first-order issue—how and why does our political-bureaucratic system decide what is vital and what is not? By whom, in what manner, and for what reasons was it decided that all Vietnam must not fall into Communist hands?

Gelb's diagnosis is partially correct: "The U. S. political-bureaucratic system did not fail; it worked." The trouble is in his implication that the "dominoes" are fictitious and therefore that Vietnam was detachable and its loss, in the last analysis, not objectively important. His prescriptions— the "new answers and new policies"—fall correspondingly short: presidential reeducation of the bureaucracy about "what is vital or important or unimportant," and "a change in general political attitudes," meaning only giving up indiscriminate "anti-Communism"—as if these had been the problems. But what if the "dominoes" are real, in several

senses, including the simple sense that it is more difficult
to defend each state if its neighbor has fallen to a hostile
and expansive power? And what if Vietnam was more than
"a civil war and a war for national independence," but a
real strategic challenge? It could matter if a piece of territory and an allied government are lost—either in themselves
or in their consequences for our position and prestige elsewhere, in the immediate region or in the world.

This does not argue for intervention, escalation, and perseverance in Vietnam. The larger point is just the opposite.
If Vietnam did matter, and yet intervention was not feasible
in Vietnam and is becoming increasingly infeasible for the
United States in general, then the lesson is more stark than
Gelb has described, and we must consider an even more
far-reaching change than Gelb has prescribed. We may
have to give up more than some supposedly fictional dominoes; we may have to give up some things in the world that
are quite real and do matter.

There is a certain immediate impression of affinity between Gelb's analysis of Vietnam and that of Daniel Ellsberg.[6] Ellsberg also explicitly rejects the "quagmire myth"—
the previously reigning paradigm of Arthur M. Schlesinger,
Jr.,[7] which postulated "inadvertence" and "one more step"
("Each step in the deepening of the American commitment
was reasonably regarded at the time as the last that would
be necessary").[8] Ellsberg also believes the choices were
deliberate, and cites two factors: ". . . the roles both of the
bureaucracy and, more importantly it seems to me, of the
U. S. domestic political system, including the special role
of the President." According to Ellsberg, "the President's
role was not passive, 'inadvertent,' nonresponsible; it did
not merely reflect bureaucratic pressures, or optimistic reporting, or assurances of the adequacy of his chosen course.
. . . What stood out from among the internal documents
was the President's personal responsibility for the particular
policy chosen." As for the role of information: "Indeed, in
each of those crisis years [1950, 1954–1955, 1961, late 1964,

early 1965]—in contrast to the years in-between—there had been enough realistic intelligence analyses and even operational reporting available to the President that it was hard to imagine that *more* truth-telling or even pessimism would have made any difference to his choices."

Here Ellsberg's critique begins to diverge. Where Gelb moves toward the proportional critique, Ellsberg moves from this analysis toward the position of the fundamentalists. As he says at the outset of his book: "In that time [seven years] I have seen [Vietnam] first as a problem; then as a stalemate; then as a crime." (These are, respectively, roughly the instrumental, the proportional, and the fundamental positions.) "As I reread now my analyses written before mid-1969—and the writings of other strategic analysts, as well as official statements—I am struck by their tacit, unquestioned belief that we had had a *right* to 'win,' in ways defined by us (i.e., by the President); or, at least, a right to prolong a war, to 'avoid defeat'; or at very worst, to lose only gracefully, covertly, slowly: all these, even the last, at the cost of an uncounted number of Asian lives, a toll to which our policy set no real limit." In short, all the other critiques of the war retained American national interests as the objective, without admitting the cost in Vietnamese lives and property as a constraint to all. To Ellsberg, Vietnam was "a wholly illegitimate unilateral intervention, desperately unwanted by most of those of another nation and culture, designed to determine who should govern them, how they should live, and which of them should die. . . . It was what 'extreme' critics—and most international lawyers— had been saying about the nature of our involvement for years. I had not believed them. Now I had to."

The fundamentalist position typically is founded on two premises: (1) the attribution of immorality, even crimes, and (2) the call for thorough, even revolutionary, institutional change. Although this position may evoke some sympathetic vibrations, it has logical as well as practical problems. When drawn out strictly, each of the two legs of the fundamentalist case has difficult implications; when taken together, they present something of a contradiction, precisely because they constitute a logical overkill.

To figure out why this is so, we have to analyze the logical structure, not just savor the plausibility, of the fundamentalist analysis and prescription. Such a pure, even abstract, analysis risks oversimplification, but empirical content and complexity can be added back after the logical structure of the argument has been clarified. Logical analysis is not a mere intellectual sport. The logic of a situation affects what we propose to do about it; the answer is surely not to do just anything, or everything. In any case, logical analysis provides a way to test an explanatory model for its relevance to policy. The test is to examine the prescriptions that are generated from it by logical extension.

The fundamentalists attempt to explain America's decisions to wage counterrevolutionary intervention and destructive war by, first, imputing criminality and immorality to the American leadership. This must be understood as a *necessary condition*. According to the fundamentalists, (1) the decisions involved crimes, (2) the decision makers were aware of the crimes, and (3) they made these decisions anyway. This conjunction of facts means that morality and legality failed to operate as constraints on the decisions to intervene and escalate; the very fact that there was intervention implies that there were immoral and illegal decisions. In propositional shorthand, this assertion is: if intervention, then immorality. Or it can be stated in the form of its converse: if no immorality, then no intervention; or (the more normal statement of a necessary condition), only if immorality, then intervention. The prescriptive remedy appears as a sufficient condition:[9] The operation or the restoration of morality should lead to nonintervention. In propositional shorthand, again: if morality, then no intervention.[10] In other words, the imputation of crime or immorality as a necessary condition for destructive intervention implies that, if these were absent, the limits on intervention would be tighter and more reliable, and the results in future cases would be more humane. These, in fact, are the analysis and remedy to which Daniel Ellsberg subscribed at least in his analysis of Vietnam in 1972; they seem also to have been the principle on which he acted in revealing the Pentagon Papers.

The second fundamentalist condition is that counter-revolutionary intervention is the inevitable result of capitalist institutions. This must be understood as a *sufficient condition* (given a certain external situational challenge). This second condition can be seen as the extreme statement of Gelb's proposition that "the system worked" in the case of Vietnam. The prescriptive remedy appears as a necessary condition:[11] Only by radically changing the institutional premises of the American economy, society, polity, and bureaucracy can we bring about a change in our international objectives and methods. In propositional shorthand, again: only if no capitalist institutions, then no intervention. (This does not mean, of course, that doing away with capitalist institutions will guarantee the elimination of intervention; there might be other sufficient conditions and therefore other necessary remedies.) This portion of the fundamentalist thesis, embraced by the radical left, was rejected by Ellsberg, as we shall see, at least in the special context of prescribing a sufficiently quick end to the Vietnam war.

Now, logically these two parts of the fundamentalist case (immorality and capitalist institutions) stand in contradiction to each other (not that either, in particular, is thereby rendered false). If one proposition is a necessary condition, the other can hardly be a sufficient condition. The first proposition (that immorality is a ncecessary condition for intervention) preempts the second (that capitalist institutions are a sufficient condition for intervention); and the second porposition obviates the first. The remedies appropriate to these two different kinds of analysis (the moral and the economic-institutional) are also mutually contradic-

tory, but in reverse: morality is held to be a sufficient
remedy, but radical institutional change is held to be a
necessary remedy.

The fundamentalists could perhaps have asserted that
either of the conditions, immorality or capitalist institutions,
is sufficient to produce destructive intervention; in that case
both remedies, morality and institutional change, would
together be necessary. Or they could have asserted that
both of the propositions together are necessary; in that case
either remedy would be sufficient in itself. In fact, in much
this fashion, the fundamentalists often overstate their case.
The effects of such redundant analysis are seen mostly in
the prescribed remedies: (1) Piling up necessary conditions
makes *any* remedy sufficient and the others not needed.
Thus a case can be trivialized. (2) Piling up sufficient conditions makes *every* remedy necessary. This can become
(in Ellsberg's words) "a counsel of despair." And, as we
have seen, (3) juxtaposing necessary and sufficient conditions, and thus remedies, leads to contradictions. Perhaps
sensing these logical difficulties, fundamentalist critics tend
to oscillate between postulating the sufficiency of automatic
institutional determinism and postulating the necessity of
deliberate immoral conspiracy.

A general conclusion is that, in deriving lessons from
history, one should be careful not to be too multicausal,
identifying factors or roots for the sake of amassing points
in the style of the lawyer's brief, rather than identifying
structure for the sake of revealing essential relationships
in the manner of the political analyst. The object of historical analysis, to use a mechanical analogy, should be
to reconstruct a perfectly operational watch (or model),
leaving half the parts (or propositions) on the table. In
this case, more can be less. The immediate point is that the
fundamentalists can't really have it both ways: They can
have the moral premise or the institutional premise, but
not both.

Even the individual premises of the fundamentalists,

however, taken separately, are not ultimately constructive in the search for efficacious remedies. I find their first assertion—immorality as a necessary condition for intervention—to be a blind alley. The search for villains may uncover some real ones, but that is beside the point. It is entirely plausible that in future cases, for seemingly proper and even benign reasons, right-minded persons (much more right-minded than those Ellsberg asserts were making decisions on Vietnam between 1950 and 1973) would come to much the same strategic choices. The first, or moral, argument does not ask enough of the analysis and consequently promises too much of the proposed remedy.

I find the second element of the fundamentalist argument—capitalist institutions as a sufficient condition for intervention—also to be a blind alley because it searches in a wrong (and practically hopeless) place for the sources of constructive change. The second, or institutional, argument asserts too much in the analysis and consequently asks too much of the remedy—and, incidentally, promises too little, since the elimination of capitalist institutions would still leave other potential sufficient conditions for repressive interventions.[12]

For much the same reasons, Ellsberg himself did not—at least in his argument in *Papers on the War* in 1972[13]—accept this second fundamentalist doctrine and prescription for change: "Have I, recently, only imagined an America that 'could'—*short of* [italics added] radical change in its own society and politics—change itself to abandon counterrevolution in Vietnam and elsewhere, as once I imagined American and Saigon governments that could master it? That is one position on the Left. It could be correct; yet it is a counsel of despair—which I am not ready to accept—with respect to the fate of the people of Indochina, whose remaining social structures could be destroyed before another Presidential term is over." Ellsberg thus stopped short of the proposition that, if the system could not be totally changed, we could not end that particular destructive war.

But Ellsberg did embrace the moral argument of the fundamentalists. In fact, having rejected the institutional argument, at least for the ongoing Vietnam war, his analysis relied almost solely on the imputation of immoral, indeed criminal, behavior to American decision makers, and specifically to a succession of presidents. In this case, then, he was led to hope that a moral regeneration—perhaps to be initiated by the revelation of the Pentagon Papers—would be sufficient to curtail an illicit foreign policy and a destructive intervention: "[The Vietnamese] hope of survival as a people must rest on the possibility of a different sort of radical change, in the behavior of individuals *within* our existing, highly imperfect institutions: however urgent it is, on a longer time scale, that those institutions themselves be changed. To be radical is to go to roots; and in Dwight Macdonald's phrase 'the root is man.' The stalemated killing 'machine,' so far as there is one, is made of men and women, of human habits and relationships that they have made or maintained, and that can be unmade by them. In releasing the Pentagon Papers I acted in hope I still hold: that truths that changed me could help Americans free themselves and other victims from our longest war."

In considering the future beyond Vietnam, despite his provisional reluctance to accept institutional change as a necessary condition for reform, there are intimations, in Ellsberg's analysis, of the necessity of some institutional change. If the bureaucracy is to be dissuaded from acting as "good Germans" (significantly, Ellsberg invokes the confession of the Nazi Albert Speer[14]), a quasi-institutional solution is needed. Those who come to disagree with the moral foundations of a war must acquire the means to make their voices heard within the decision-making system or nothing will change. Ellsberg's postulate, that "only Congress and the public" can make a difference and that they must find their conscience,[15] makes sense and has effect only if our larger political system, or its distribution of weights, is changed. Ellsberg implies as much in asking that the presidency, as an institution, be shorn of some of the imperial features that it has acquired, especially in the area of foreign policy making.

We see that rejecting the theory that Vietnam was a mistake can lead to several different positions: (1) the higher-order mistake theory (the "dominoes," the indiscriminate "anti-Communism") of Gelb, (2) the fundamentalism of Ellsberg, or (3) a consistent macrostrategic analysis and a categorical prescription of nonintervention—the approach that I will propose.

In contradistinction to the fundamental critique, the strategic critique does not depend on a modern version of the devil theory—either the moral or the institutional versions.[16] I believe that America's interventionist responses *were* essentially responses, not initiatives. Furthermore, they appeared to decision makers to be necessary counters to strategic challenge; in not responding, we would have suffered some damage to our interests, even to some security interests. My conclusion is that we must have not only a different calculus of national interests but also a more restricted definition of national security. We must also have an alteration of our basic strategic "categories"—the deep cognitive mind-sets imbedded in our decision-making system—that determine how we interpret threats and how we construe necessary responses.

Lessons have to do with what we must change in order to produce correct decisions and actions in future cases that will differ in certain degrees and respects from the case at hand. Thus we have to start looking at the decisions to intervene and escalate in Vietnam not as mistakes but as choices that were made for reasons that seemed good and in circumstances that seemed compelling.

Looking at these decisions as choices rather than mistakes neither indicts nor exonerates. Rather, it draws attention to the objective logic of policy choice and the compulsions and constraints of the policy process. It concentrates on the basic strategic presumptions about threats and interests which, invoked by particular challenges, make the choices seem necessary. It is these strategic presumptions that must be changed.

PART III

FIVE ALTERNATIVE
CRITIQUES

CHAPTER 5

The Establishment's Response:
Better Instruments

Constraints and Adjustments

A nation learns from its history and adjusts to its experience in two distinct but related ways. The first is the obvious way: what the policy-making system—and, more particularly, a nation's elites—think they have learned, what they intend to do "next time." This could take the form of attitudes and resolutions about how, where, when, and even why they should fight the next war. These orientations help to shape the national disposition to future contingencies and thus constitute a significant part of what is meant by *policy*.

The second way is sometimes elusive because it is embedded in what the nation is actually doing—how its political system, its economy, its society, its organizations (including the military), and its institutions and bureaucracies are actually adjusting to the real constraints caused or accentuated by a protracted national experience such as the Vietnam

war. Though such adjustments are usually considered consequences of the events a nation has lived through, they are
also lessons. These tangible, or concrete, or existential lessons are also part of a nation's policy. They condition the
future choices of a nation by disposing the policy process—
sometimes by creating new capabilities that will enable or
tempt decision makers to use them, sometimes by creating
new constraints that will prevent or inhibit decision makers
from taking certain actions or insure that these actions will
be aborted even if they are initiated.

Some of the most important lessons of the past several
decades are of this second, tangible, type: new forms of
military organization, new patterns of deployment, new
doctrines and weapons systems, an altered civil-military
relationship. In sum, they comprise the way the nation will
allow itself to be mobilized to project its resources and
energies in other conflicts in the future.

More than the other types of critiques, the instrumental
response to Vietnam is itself a combination of the two
senses of lesson and an embodiment of their interaction.

Instrumentalism, the first of five alternative types of lessons or reaction syndromes, is a partial response to the
contradictions between foreign policy objectives and the
constraints and pressures revealed in the Vietnam war. The
instrumentalist critics adhere to the purposes and main
themes of American diplomacy but search for more efficient
means to project U. S. power. Their proposed solutions
characteristically take the form of quick fixes or compre-
hensible trade-offs—fiscal, technological, organizational, doctrinal. Even the policy changes proposed by instrumentalists
tend to be conceived as narrow trade-offs of means (though
they may have far-reaching implications). This group of
analysts is always most strongly represented in the administration—any administration—and among the permanent
bureaucracy and the military, whose daily concern is keeping the system running.

Instrumentalism is not confined to an incumbent administration. It is shared by many alumni and external critics who do not wish to inspire doubts about their commitment to the national interest and their fitness to serve again in policy-making positions. The numbers of the instrumentalists include also those in the Congress whose policy horizons are limited to investigations of cost overruns and program mismanagement. Though sometimes rightly critical of expensive weapons systems and large troop deployments abroad, the instrumentalists may be overreceptive to budgetary fixes that pare down conventional capabilities and result either in inability to meet defense commitments or in residual reliance on tactical or strategic nuclear weapons.

The national security structures of the 1960s have given way to new forms. At the root of the change have been some stringent constraints: fiscal realities, public attitudes, and the international political-military environment. Conforming to these constraints on resources and support, certain intermediate adjustments have occurred in the size and composition of defense budgets, types of armed forces, and procedures of foreign policy decision making. Because of these new structures and processes, civil-military patterns have changed, and a style of foreign policy has been adopted that looks more discriminating and restrained but may possibly harbor some surprising reactions. (This description in itself suggests, or constitutes, a partial model of policy choice. A graphic illustration of this model appears in Figure 1.)

It is interesting to gauge how far we have come. In the 1960s, the prominent features of the American national security complex were: (1) large defense budgets, swollen by the costs of an extravagantly conducted war; (2) general public and congressional support for defense programs, especially at the beginning of the period when John Kennedy came to office on the issue of a supposed national security gap; (3) large conventional forces—ground divisions, tactical air wings, and surface naval units; (4) a far-flung inventory of military installations for staging, air strikes,

Figure 1: A Model of Policy Choice

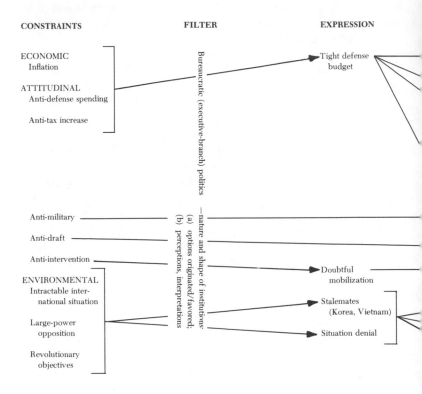

CONSTRAINTS   FILTER   EXPRESSION

Notes:

1. The model is

(a) partial: it is primarily a constraint model: it assumes a substantive structure of choice, an initial set of policy objects, and a direction of preference;

(b) qualitative: it traces the main paths, but has no coefficients and no correlation percentages;

(c) qualified: the categories are not blank, but contain indications of the nature, or direction, of the effects;

(d) situational: it describes a certain situation, rather than all situations in the abstract;

(e) political: it includes some economic terms (e.g., inflation, defense spending), but only as they function in the political process; the economic terms could be abstracted from this model and input to a model of the economy as such;

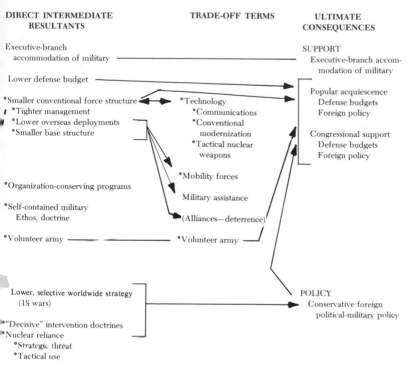

DIRECT INTERMEDIATE RESULTANTS	TRADE-OFF TERMS	ULTIMATE CONSEQUENCES

Executive-branch
  accommodation of military

Lower defense budget

°Smaller conventional force structure
°Tighter management
°Lower overseas deployments
°Smaller base structure

°Organization-conserving programs

°Self-contained military
  Ethos, doctrine

°Volunteer army

°Technology
°Communications
°Conventional
  modernization
°Tactical nuclear
  weapons

°Mobility forces

Military assistance

(Alliances—deterrence)

°Volunteer army

SUPPORT
Executive-branch accom-
  modation of military

Popular acquiescence
Defense budgets
Foreign policy

Congressional support
Defense budgets
Foreign policy

Lower, selective worldwide strategy
  (1½ wars)

°"Decisive" intervention doctrines
°Nuclear reliance
  °Strategic threat
  °Tactical use

POLICY
Conservative foreign
  political-military policy

(f) redundant: some terms are carried forward and appear in two columns (e.g., tactical nuclear weapons as a direct intermediate resultant and a trade-off term; executive-branch accommodation of military as a direct intermediate resultant and an ultimate consequence).

2. The prefixed symbol ° indicates characteristics of the new military structure, whether they are direct intermediate resultants or trade-off terms.

Source: Earl C. Ravenal, editor and co-author, *Peace with China? U. S. Decisions for Asia* (New York: Liveright, 1971).

naval repairs, logistics, communications, and intelligence, creating a world-wide U. S. presence; (5) an industrial system heavily committed, directly or indirectly, to military uses, causing large-scale depletion of the civil industrial base through the diversion of critical skills, research effort, and capital;[1] (6) a subtle but pervasive militarization of society through the installation of military training facilities and the sponsorship of defense research in the midst of educational establishments, ubiquitous draft calls, and the glorification of military commanders (illustrated by the brief apotheosis of General Westmoreland, when he was transiently able to promise a quick military victory in Vietnam); (7) widespread academic preference for military solutions to foreign policy problems and for Machiavellian psychopolitical manipulation, and an acme of prestige for "think tanks" and "defense intellectuals"; (8) the accession of influential military figures, such as General Maxwell Taylor, to commanding positions in White House decision making; and (9) above all, a skewed set of priorities that gave primary support to world-wide political-military maneuvering at the expense of domestic welfare.

The premises of this situation have changed. Though some of the policies and structures of the 1960s endure and some of the critics are still obsessed with their original evidence and paradigms, it is fair to say that we now have a different set of tendencies. Most of these changes occurred during the Nixon-Kissinger regime, and they have largely persisted into the Carter administration, despite some eddies in the continuing current.

What have been the adjustments—we might call them "existential" lessons of Vietnam—in the popular and institutional constraints, the force structures, budget limits and decision rules, and the new civil-military and foreign policy dispensations? The most important of these concrete lessons is that the American public will not tolerate either a long, costly conflict or a large peacetime military force that appears to have only limited utility in solving this country's external problems.[2] This is not equivalent to the judgment that the American economy cannot stand such expenditures. It can absorb several times the expense of such efforts, if the economy and the emotional support of the nation are mobilized.[3] But this would require a more obvious and central threat to the country's security. So the operative constraint is the practical denial of mobilization, in most circumstances. Indeed, during the Vietnam war, the government's self-imposed decision rule of "no mobilization" was one of the most inhibiting constraints on the conduct of the war. President Johnson relied on the draft and the creation of new units in July 1965 and refrained from calling up the Army Ready Reserve Force, partially because of the unfavorable public reaction to President Kennedy's use of this force during the Berlin crisis of 1961. Had Johnson declared a state of emergency and issued a general call-up of reserves in 1965, an earlier test of the public's support for the Vietnam war would have been precipitated.[4] The critical point is that the restraint is self-imposed because it is politically perceived; it reflects the judgment of the national leadership that the public cannot be taxed or mobilized to fight an indecisive peripheral war or to provide large peacetime conventional forces.

A second general influence on our national security structures is the change in public attitudes toward the profession of arms. Public disapproval of the military may come in independent cycles. Or it may be a normal historical revulsion toward the warriors even of a successful conflict, let alone a disastrous or indecisive or aborted one. Or we may be seeing an expression of a secular evolution of attitudes away from the violent resolution of international disputes. But whether it is independently cyclical, or a lagged reaction to war or a certain kind of war, or a continuously evolving public sentiment—or some overlay of several of all of these factors—a certain antimilitary feeling became evident during the long involvement in Vietnam. (With the end of American involvement in Southeast Asia, however, the crisis of this reaction seems to have passed.)

A third major determinant of a profoundly altered American military and foreign policy is the increasing intractability of the international system. It is not clear how American conventional military power will be profitably, or even successfully, employed, especially in areas that are contested by large powers.

These domestic and international constraints determine the size and nature of American forces and the strategies planned for their employment and, in turn, our eventual civil-military relationships and foreign policies.

Trade-Offs and Quick Fixes

The first of these constraints resulting from Vietnam, popular resistance to interminable war or extravagant forces, expressed itself primarily in the form of budgetary stringency and occasioned a series of instrumental changes: a smaller, relatively cheaper force structure,[5] a more controlled scope and quicker determination of future American military actions, more tightly managed procurement and operation of weapons systems and forces, and acceptance of some cost-compelled deficiencies in military capabilities—a compromise between the need for budget cuts and the desire of the senior military to keep intact the organizational framework of their services.

The physical expression of this development is more technological and more mobile forces.[6] Many of the specific developments have been the results of product testing in the laboratory of Vietnam.[7] Some innovations center on close tactical air support, which enjoyed relatively little official interest and resources until the beginning of the Vietnam war but was developed to a potent military art during that conflict. The principal types of close air support were the classic fighter-bomber, the slow but heavily armed "platforms" such as the AC-47 and the AC-130, the helicopter gunship, and the conventionally configured B-52 bomber. Vietnam also spawned a revolution in tactical mobility, with new doctrine, command techniques, and organizational form (the airmobile division) developed around utility, supply, observation, and gunship helicopters. Gadgets such as night vision devices and "people-sniffers" were also tested and deployed. The Navy learned to operate as a riverine force. The Marines geared up to fight sustained campaigns on land and developed more integral logistics. Precision guidance devices, such as "smart" (television- and laser-guided) bombs, were evolved by the Air Force and Navy in the bombing campaigns against North Vietnam.

The salient technological lessons of Vietnam were sophisticated and comprehensive information and response systems, approximating the "automated battlefield" envisioned by senior Army commanders.[8] This concept was glowingly unveiled by General Westmoreland in October 1969 at the annual meeting of the Association of the U. S. Army. It had been proposed originally, in August 1966, by a committee of scientists at the Institute for Defense Analyses (an adjunct of the Office of the Secretary of Defense) as an electronic barrier to inhibit infiltration across the demilitarized zone in Vietnam—a complex of audio, seismic, and magnetic sensors, airborne and other signal-pickup devices, computer deciphering equipment, and fast-reaction aircraft and artillery fire. This proposal was sanctioned by Secretary of Defense McNamara and promptly became known as the Mc-Namara Line. It became a reality on the ground in Vietnam in the winter of 1967–1968. The electronic battlefield concept eventually included three variants: the fixed ground barrier near the DMZ (the McNamara Line itself), the air-supported systems in Laos ("Igloo White"), and the tactical applications in South Vietnam by individual land-force units (as in the sieges at Khe Sanh and various remote firebases). Although the McNamara Line itself was discontinued within a year, the other two concepts continued and were considered by military and congressional reviewers to be technically effective. The electronic battlefield may, in the future, include the deployment of remotely piloted vehicles (RPVs) by the Air Force (fixed-wing aircraft) and the Army (rotary-wing aircraft). By the end of fiscal year 1971, electronic battlefield programs, including research by the Army (the STANO and MASSTER programs) and the Air Force and Navy, had already cost $3.5 billion.

Another technological orientation occasioned by Vietnam has been a renewed interest in tactical nuclear weapons, with efforts to invent appropriate applications and doctrine. During the 1960s, relatively little research, doctrinal development, or training had occurred in the tactical nuclear area. But at the end of that decade, and in the early to mid-1970s, revealing suggestions appeared in the strategic literature, both inside and outside the military services. Some influential commentators on U.S. national security policy have become aware of a contradiction of commitments and resources and would like to resolve it by reliance on tactical nuclear weapons. An example is C. L. Sulzberger, who approvingly quotes an article by Robert M. Lawrence: "We [the U. S.] will either have to increase our ability to respond to local threats, or in the future we will have to see a substantial reduction in our commitments and influence over the course of events. In the aftermath of Vietnam, we certainly do not propose to fight a large-scale conventional war with China. Yet the ability to engage Chinese military forces successfully may be a *sine qua non* of deterrence and stability in Asia." Sulzberger concludes: "The answer may well lie in the field of truly tactical atomic weapons."[9]

Another example is the speech of former Deputy Secretary of Defense David Packard before the Europe-America Conference in Amsterdam in March 1973, in which he pointed out the potential effectiveness of relatively clean "mini nukes" delivered with high precision guidance. Mini-nukes also enjoyed the support of General Andrew J. Goodpaster while he was supreme commander of allied forces in Europe: "If we were to apply in a controlled way limited numbers of nuclear weapons sufficient simply to stop [a large-scale nonnuclear Soviet attack on Western Europe] and impose costs and losses on their attack echelons, my own feeling is that the probabilities would be much less than even that they would immediately carry that to all-out nuclear exchange involving their own homeland."[10] There have also been other references to small atomic weapons ("Pentagon plans to develop a new generation of miniature atomic weapons with less radioactive fallout") that would be useful, not particularly for deterrence, but in the actual conduct of a war. Former Assistant Secretary of Defense Alain C. Enthoven testified that "the Pentagon rationale for developing small, 'clean' tactical weapons for U. S. Pershing missiles is that they would be effective against military targets while sparing civilian areas from massive destruction."[11]

The possible future use of tactical nuclear weapons depends not only on technological preparations but also on the propensity of the American military to use them. In this respect, Drew Middleton's judgment is interesting: "The prevailing view among senior American and allied commanders is that the East's quantitative and qualitative superiority over NATO is so great that the West would be forced to use tactical nuclear weapons to prevent the quick conquest of West Germany, France, the Netherlands and Belgium. They believe, then, that military preparation and planning should aim for success in a tactical nuclear war with 'the most probable adversary,' the Soviet Union."[12] Still another indication is an article in *Air University Review*, which summarizes the authoritative current *U. S. Air Force Basic Doctrine*: "Low-intensity nuclear operations (formerly tactical nuclear operations) constitute an area of significant development. The major philosophical shift concerns the use of low-yield nuclear weapons and the limited use of larger nuclear weapons."[13]

Early and primary use of nuclear weapons is also advocated in an Army source, which severely criticizes the prevailing doctrine of "flexible response" and the "pause" on the grounds that this could only favor the Soviets. It suggests not only the early use, but even the preemptive use, of tactical nuclear weapons. It expects that these might be employed in a controlled and rational manner, confined to the immediate battlefield. And it favors the devolution of their control to national military authorities to promote the efficiency and credibility of their use.[14] Other recent advocates of a significant tactical nuclear strategy have been: Colin S. Gray, who argues for a nuclear defensive doctrine for NATO;[15] W. S. Bennett, R. R. Sandoval, and R. G. Shreffler;[16] Philip A. Karber;[17] James H. Polk;[18] and Joseph I. Coffey, who argues for a U. S. NATO policy that would "favor concepts for the quick (if limited) employment of nuclear weapons against large-scale assaults, rather than those calling for protracted conventional operations."[19] And finally, Secretary of Defense Rumsfeld, in his annual posture statement for FY 1977, acknowledged: "During the past few years the U. S. theater nuclear force (TNF) posture has received increasing attention, both outside and within the Defense Department. Concerns have centered on our policy for employment and deployment of these nuclear weapons as well as on their security and survivability" (p. 98).[20]

During the 1960s, relatively little research, doctrinal development, or training had occurred in the tactical nuclear area. It is significant now that many of the intellectual middle-grade officers, those who are capable of drawing and projecting lessons from the Vietnam experience, have been more forward in calling for a renewed examination of this means of asserting America's comparative advantage in capital-intensive, high-technology warmaking. Vietnam was a more focused frustration for these military professionals than for the nation as a whole. They developed a disgust for the retrograde cowboys and Indians approaches fashioned in the early 1960s to cope with insurgencies and guerrilla wars and an impatience with fighting the enemy not only on his own ground but on his own level and terms.[21]

Are there overwhelming psychological and political inhibitions on the use of tactical nuclear weapons by an American president? Some points must be kept in mind when assessing the propensity of a president to depart from proportionality and respect for international political risks. (1) A president might be responsive to a strong and articulate faction on the American political scene; specifically, he might act in fear of his right wing. (2) He might set a policy unilaterally, without going through the full process of consultation with the interested members of the international community, as in the "Nixon shocks" to Japan in July and August 1971 (particularly the trade and monetary restrictions of August 15) and the nuclear alert during the Middle East war of October 1973. (3) He might, in the process of justifying his policy and strengthening his hand, invoke public support for severe and decisive action—support that later would be hard to manage or mitigate.

Thus, future American military initiatives could be unilateral, narrowly motivated, disproportionate, and heedless of international reactions. Especially in the area of security measures, the very nature of the acts and the rigid requirements of secrecy preclude much consultation, even within our own government. (The invasion of Cambodia in 1970, the resumption of aggressive air strikes on North Vietnam, the raid at Sontay,[22] the mining of Haiphong, the Christmas 1972 bombing of Hanoi, and the worldwide nuclear alert of October 1973 are cases in support of this point.) As for consultation with Congress, the most likely procedure is that a few reliable members will be selectively briefed and so implicated in an essentially presidential act.[23]

So far, we have noted that budgetary constraints can produce more technologically sophisticated forces and a penchant for military actions intended to be decisive, including the use of nuclear weapons. Another consequence of budgetary stringency is a leaner base structure, both within the continental United States and abroad. Under budgeting pressure, Pentagon managers have implemented proposals for efficiency reductions and consolidations that had been, in fatter times, indignantly rejected.[24]

An indirect consequence of overseas troop reductions and base closures would logically be the further development of intertheater mobility—ways of getting centrally located forces mobilized, transported overseas, and deployed. (For various reasons, however, strategic mobility remains inadequate to compensate for force reductions overseas.) A concomitant of mobility, essential to its feasibility, is the readiness of reserve forces, both the active units that are held centrally for conflicts at the periphery and the forces in cadre or inactive form, variously trained and equipped and embedded in the civilian economy. Since mobilization of inactive units causes economic dislocations and arouses political resentment, it has been considered an undesirable expedient. These inadequacies of strategic mobility and force readiness are themselves indications of the limits of "instrumental" solutions to our national security problems.

Antimilitary feeling, the second major factor that emerged from the Vietnam War, had some early consequences. One was the defensive reaction of the military professionals who embody the standards and determine the conduct and structure of their organizations. The effects have been a smaller, more reliable cadre and a narrower conception of military professionalism. There has also been a psychological deflection of criticism from outside; in some ways this is a justified response to misdirected hostility from civilian society, which attempted to fasten its frustrations on those to whom it had delegated its international dirty work. Such a reaction was apparent in the sympathy of many army officers for Lieutenant Calley during his trial for the crimes of Mylai.[25]

The advent of the all-volunteer Army completes in depth the professionalism of the services. The ultimate success of this draft-free Army depends on the continuation of high military pay scales, low manpower quotas, and high unemployment levels in the civilian economy. It is far from certain that all these conditions, especially the last, will be met over the long haul. The six-month trial period between the practical end of the draft (December 1972) and the formal expiration of conscription (July 1973) demonstrated an increasing shortfall between manpower requirements and enlistments;[26] though, by mid-1975, enlistment quotas were oversubscribed, largely because of the soft economic situation.

Nor is it settled that, even if the conditions were met, a volunteer Army would be an unmixed blessing. Some have feared that a volunteer Army would be a force of socially isolated mercenaries, more amenable to presidential adventures, and that a budget-constricted and manpower-deficient force might encourage its commanders to rely on nuclear weapons. Other criticisms are that the volunteer force will be composed disproportionately of blacks, particularly in the combat arms,[27] and that the steep pay increases necessary to inspire enlistment have pushed manpower costs to well over half the defense budget, prejudicing expenditures on research, modernization, and sufficient quantities of weapons.[28]

The end of conscription has also reduced incentives for individuals to join the reserves or the National Guard, leading to severe deficits in the strength of those units. And demographic forecasts indicate serious shortages in the age-pools from which the future volunteer Army will have to be recruited.[29] All of these analyses and projections have inspired calls for a return to some kind of conscription, "perhaps a form of universal service, civilian and military without exemptions."[30]

The classic criticism of a completely professional military force is that it would inevitably develop its own alienated ethos, peculiar protective traditions, involuted loyalty, and neutrality of purpose. Such an organization might even acquire some of the characteristics of a praetorian guard, available to do a president's bidding efficiently abroad in exchange for certain immunities and privileges at home.

The breach of such an implied bargain in some future crisis, foreign or domestic, might—remotely—bring America closer to the extremity of the French Fourth Republic.[31]

The third major determinant to emerge from Vietnam is the prospect of the frustration of American intervention. Our strategists and policy makers have already made certain responses to this fact and this prospect, in the form of some of the instrumental changes mentioned above—new weapons, force structures, and directions of research and development, and a more professional military establishment.

American strategists have also responded by basing military action on different psychological and political premises. The large and frustrating engagements fought by the United States since the Second World War—Korea and Vietnam—are sometimes taken as invalidating the respect for territorial sanctuaries. That is one conclusion, but not the primary one. Most analysts recognize that extending the conflict by bombing Manchuria or invading North Vietnam would have brought only severe attrition of U. S. air or ground forces and indefinite involvement; the incursion into Cambodia precipitated a larger disaster. Thus, placing territorial limits on American escalation is still accepted as a constraint. Rather, Korea and Vietnam are more widely taken, among influential and practical groups, as discrediting the doctrine of measured and progressive application of conventional force. In this reading, the few "successful" uses of American military power since the Second World War have been the Taiwan Strait conflict in 1958 and the Cuban missile crisis in 1962—big power confrontations that were resolved by nuclear threats—and the Lebanon landing in 1958 and the Dominican Republic occupation in 1965— small-power situations that were smothered by sudden overwhelming mobile interventions.

In fact, one of the most widely accepted instrumental lessons among national security elites is the notion that future interventions must be sudden, central, and (in one way or another) overwhelming. A recent article by an Ameri-

can naval officer is indicative: "The truth is . . . that we could
have won the war, and without greater destruction. . . . From
the outset of our direct involvement, we had the air power
and the naval power to destroy the North Vietnam capacity
to fight. . . . We could have struck them before they had
established their air defense, we could have extended our
naval bombardment deep into the north at once, and we
could have mined Haiphong harbor . . . [in] a strong, sustained, and decisive attack in the North in 1965."[32]

Significant also is the response to a survey of 2,280
American foreign policy practitioners and academics.[33]
When asked to comment on the proposition, "If foreign
interventions are undertaken, the necessary force should
be applied in a short period of time rather than through a
policy of graduated escalation," 78% agreed, and the percentage that responded "agree strongly" (49%) was the
largest of any of the questions asked.

In this respect, the comments of Secretary of Defense
James R. Schlesinger, referring to a possible attack on South
Korea, were also revealing: "One of the lessons of the Vietnamese conflict is that rather than simply counter your opponents' thrusts, it is necessary to go for the heart of the
opponents' power: destroy his military forces rather than
simply being involved endlessly in ancillary military operations."[34]

Consequences of the Instrumental Reaction

The post-Vietnam American national security establishment, for all its continuing extravagance, is now relatively
smaller and more remote, impinging less on the ordinary
life of the nation. As a consequence, we have already seen
the return to a civil-military relationship characterized by
tacit public toleration. This may not be warm support but
rather a kind of "amilitarism."[35] Indeed, during the Watergate scandal (fall 1973), in comparison with civilian institutions that were then considered corrupt or impotent (the
Presidency, the Congress), the military was rated the most

admired American institution, by the standard of "how well they serve the country."[36]

In return, the American defense structure and capacity for response will be less dependent on public enthusiasm for the military organizations or even on public apprehension of external threat. In one possible scenario, a new concordat may be established: a low profile foreign policy and a volunteer Army are sustained. These moves appeal to the motives of a satisfied and privileged nation. The majority of American middle-class youth, untroubled by conscription, reverts to its basic social conservatism, desiring only that the reward system remain stable.[37] A self-serving American labor force is pacified by the granting of some of its protectionist demands. The foreign policy community (the active bureaucracy, its alumni, and the interested public) welcomes what it sees as a more pragmatic world strategy. And a solid working majority in Congress combines a sense of fiscal responsibility with support for the supposed essentials of national security.[38] Some features of this scenario have been realized. Thus it is quite possible that, in some future extremity, a president will have considerable latitude to employ a lean, mobile, smartly managed, technologically sophisticated force, in pursuit of appropriately decisive strategic doctrines.

Also, the civilian national security bureaucracy has become more complaisant toward the military—even though, paradoxically, the overt influence of the services and the Joint Chiefs of Staff on the decision process seems to be at a low ebb.[39] For one thing, the "fiscal guidance" budgeting of the Nixon administration proved to be more neutral toward the strategic concepts of the military organizations. This acquiescence in the notions of the military produced some early institutional casualties. The Pentagon Office of Systems Analysis, which had provided secretaries of defense in the early 1960s with independent advice on major defense issues, was emasculated,[40] and has never recovered a strong, substantive, and independent influence. The Office of International Security Affairs (ISA) was also drained of its independent force and status. These two organizational shifts were achieved by several means: the bureaucratic redistribution of procedural advantages to the military agencies within the Pentagon; the recruitment of individuals with greater affinity to the positions of the services and the Joint Chiefs of Staff; and the disposition of a higher percentage of contested issues in favor of the military.

It is instructive that the recommendations of the Fitzhugh Blue Ribbon Defense Panel[41] that were totally rejected by Secretary Laird and Deputy Secretary Packard were those that would have furthered civilian control of the defense establishment: removing the command of military units in the theaters and the formulation of strategy from the hands of the Joint Chiefs of Staff, and reducing the military services to caretakers of tangible assets and operators of training establishments.[42] The only sections of the blue ribbon report to be implemented were some organizationally neutral improvements in procurement and development and some peripheral suggestions about public relations and conflicts of interest.

There has also been a corresponding instrumental change in the nature of our foreign policy. In the Nixon-Kissinger years, its whole character moved closer to a Byzantine model—more mature, more sophisticated, less ideological; premised on our ability to engineer allied contributions on the marches of empire (the Nixon Doctrine); manipulative of ally and adversary alike (balance of power diplomacy); articulating subtle threats rather than squandering actual strength. Public support for intervention was sought less fervently by the president. These features of diplomacy have, to a certain extent, been perpetuated by the Carter administration, despite the earlier criticism of many of its articulate members when out of office. Our policy, even now, depends on interventions, wherever they remain feasible. They will simply be—it is hoped—more decisive.

Thus the dominant lesson learned by the establishment

has been the instrumental one. The results have been a smaller force structure, a new civil-military balance, and a foreign policy that aims to maintain global order by proxy military forces, sharp selective interventions, and large implied threats.

CHAPTER 6

The Liberal Critique:
A Sense of Proportion

Curiously, it is American liberals who may have learned the least—though they have analyzed and criticized the most —from the American foreign policy experience of their generation. The proportional thesis became the characteristic countercritique of the liberals when the instrumental approach was the prevailing critique within the Nixon-Ford administrations. The arguments of the liberals while out of office give us a handle on their present policies, now that they have become the administration again.

The proportionalist critics include some thoughtful public servants as well as many "liberal-realist" academics. Their problem arises from the fact that many of these critics originally supported the American stand in Southeast Asia on strategic or ideological grounds; but, as the war dragged on, some defected from the policies even of the Johnson administration and many more came to oppose those of the Nixon administration. They defected largely because they

believed that the costs and the destruction had become disproportionate to the strategic results and to the value of the
American interests in the situation. The proportional critique
offered a logical—and respectable—way to climb down from
previous support for the Vietnam War while reaffirming the
feasibility of future interventions and the necessity and
morality of limited war in general. (Of course, this intellectual stance also enabled the critics to climb back up, into
office, and to execute "effective" foreign policies again.
There is more than a tinge of careerism in the proportionalist
position.)

The particular problem of the proportionalists is how to
preserve the premise of intervention when necessary but to
repudiate the case of Vietnam. The most readily available
solution is to assert that Vietnam is distinguishable from all
other cases—the historical ones and the ones likely in the
future. Thus, Vietnam is seen as peripheral and irrelevant
to the global or regional balance of power, and also as
unique and not replicable—in short, not the type of situation
in which we needed to intervene. Furthermore, the uniqueness, the peculiar character, of the Vietnam conflict is
posited as the reason for the futility of our intervention.

From a logical perspective, the proportional critique consists of a series of overlapping propositions. (1) Vietnam was
excessive (it violated the canons of limited war) because
(a) disproportionate measures (both costly for ourselves and
damaging to others) were taken (b) for objectives that were
irrelevant or not sufficiently valuable. (2) It was also *unnecessary* because it was (a) irrelevant and (b) unique (not
replicable). Finally, (3) it was *infeasible* because it was
peculiarly intractable.

The features that are taken to characterize Vietnam are:
(1) it was essentially a civil war, and (2) the communist side
had inherited a genuine anticolonial struggle (the other side
of the coin of the political debility of the Saigon regime). Of
course, these or any other features do not in themselves
settle the question of the propriety of intervention, one way

or another. For one thing, every war is a civil war in a larger sense and on some level: it is internecine and one group is trying to reverse the existing order in its favor. But the point is broader than that. The essential criteria that might determine our intervention are necessity and feasibility. Each of these criteria invokes a further set of considerations. As for necessity, what kind of value of our own is held to be at stake in the situation—security? morality? Thus, the attributes of a particular situation in themselves are less important than the values we think are challenged or threatened. As for feasibility, most people, including the proportionalists, would define this as the prospect of attaining the objective with appropriate means (that is, without excessive costs and casualties for ourselves and without unnecessary destruction of innocent, and even enemy, property and lives). Thus, even more important than the values at stake in the situation, in absolute terms, is the weighing of those values against the costs and consequences of intervention to defend them.

The proportionalists are not oblivious to these considerations of necessity and feasibility. That is why they assert that the features that characterize Vietnam are precisely those that made our intervention at once unnecessary and futile. Moreover, they go on to assert that those features also distinguish Vietnam and make unlikely the emergence of a similar case that might occasion another mistaken, and equally disastrous, intervention. The proportionalist case concludes, retrospectively, that we need not have made the mistake of intervening in Vietnam itself (though our intervention might initially have seemed justifiable; we either mistook one case for another or failed to adjust when one case became another); and, prospectively, that we should not make the opposite mistake of failing to intervene in other more worthy and amenable cases in the future.

To box the compass, let us review the four possible cases of intervention:

    A. Unnecessary and infeasible—we do not have to intervene, and could not win anyway;

    B. Unnecessary but feasible—we do not have to inter-
vene, but could win;

    C. Necessary but infeasible—we must intervene, but
cannot win;

    D. Necessary and feasible—we must intervene, and
can win.

The proportionalists allege that Vietnam is case A, in effect
a double mistake. It turns out that we did not have to intervene and could not have won anyway (within the proper
bounds). Ironically, if this is all there is to the lesson, Vietnam is not really an interesting case. It does not tell us anything about some future situation that any untutored person
on the street didn't already know—except, of course, that we
will always have the problem of identifying the future situation for what it is.

    Case B, where we do not have to intervene but could win,
is exemplified in our interventions in the Dominican Republic (1965) and perhaps Lebanon (1958)—though the decision makers of the time might not have agreed that those
interventions were inessential. Such cases might present
some moral questions about the wanton use of force, but
they present no difficult strategic problems.

    The real trouble lies in case C, where we "must" inter-
vene but cannot win. (Of course, the "must" expresses our
nation's sense of strategic necessity, not necessarily my own
judgment or an objective estimate.) The world will increasingly present us with this kind of case, and it is an excruciat-
ing dilemma. In the view of many (though not the proportionalists), this is the case that is epitomized by Vietnam.
It is certainly the case that makes Vietnam interesting, now
and in the future.

    The most subtle problem, in a way, is posed by cases like
D, where we "must" intervene and can win. Here, on its
face, intervention should command support—and does command the support of the instrumentalists, the proportionalists, and even the consequentialists. Only those whose
critical principle leads to a general presumption of non-

intervention would dissent. These would be the moral fundamentalists and the proponents of consistent strategic disengagement. The latter two positions, as we shall see, while
converging on this judgment, differ from each other in their
implications. The fundamental critique rejects even supposedly vital national interests as a justification for intervention (though it tends to regard them as a cause of
intervention). The strategic critique accepts the strategic
requisite—the "must"—but defines it quite differently and
much more restrictively.

The proportional critique is really not designed to avoid
future intervention. On the contrary, the position of the proportionalists is "intervention when necessary" and "intervention as long as feasible." To them, the presumption of
intervention is established; the doctrine of proportion only
qualifies the style of intervention, establishes a measure for
escalation, and provides a principle of practical morality.
Their insistence on the uniqueness, the nonreplicability, of
Vietnam preserves the commitment to future intervention.
It is entirely consistent with the proportionalist position to
see our intervention in Vietnam as a mistake—the mistake,
precisely, of failing to recognize the unique features of the
situation.

It is interesting in this regard that the radical left (which
tends to be fundamentalist) has never viewed Vietnam, as
the liberals have come to do, as a civil war. The left, with the
conservative right, characterizes Vietnam as a war of intervention, a struggle by larger forces on both sides for larger—
indeed, vital—stakes. According to left analysis, Vietnam was
never a mistake for the United States; for American capitalism it was always a grim necessity. Also interesting was the
preparation by administration liberals, even in the earlier
escalatory phases of the war, of an intellectual groundwork
for the special theory of Vietnam—the "atypical features,"
the "nationalist movement," the civil war—that would explain and possibly differentiate a later failure.[1]

Ironically, because of the proportionalists' sensitivity in

defining the character of the Vietnam War, they fail to generalize usefully from that situation, to draw conclusions of sufficient amplitude to provide guidance in future situations that will vary in certain respects and degrees. There is no reason to think that our future adversaries will make their challenges clear and our choices simple. There will be some entirely indigenous revolutionary wars; but there will also be many shades of ambiguous commitment by the established communist powers (the citadels of revolution, the Soviet Union and China, as well as some lesser communist nations). The diplomacy of detente and our pragmatic partial alignment with Peking may have put some limits on their behavior; there may be some tactical modifications, some restraint. But we cannot expect their behavioral modifications to include the complete disavowal of revolutionary movements.

Moreover, future challenges may not be limited to promoting indigenous insurgencies—challenges that might, conceivably, be ignored. Revisionist and revolutionary forces could perpetrate invasions in places like Korea, Thailand, the Middle East, or southern Africa. To write off Vietnam as a mistake, as the proportionalists do, is to avoid the critical questions: will the United States intervene to oppose the export of revolution (whether hard or soft), and must we structure our forces and our deterrent posture to deal with such challenges?

All the characteristic features of the proportionalist thesis —that the Vietnam war was unnecessary and infeasible, that it was a disproportionate effort for peripheral stakes in a unique and nonreplicable situation, and that our involvement was essentially a mistake—are present in the critique of George W. Ball. The proportionalist character of Ball's critique is distilled in his judgment:

> It was a tragic defeat for America . . . not because our initial purposes were unworthy but because—in frustration and false pride and our innocence of the art of extrication—we were forced to the employment of

excessively brutal means to achieve an equivocal objective against a poor, backward country.[2]

I have already mentioned Ball's stress on the unique circumstances of Vietnam.[3] Here I comment on his treatment of limited war. Ball makes the classic point about the dilemma that a democracy faces in prosecuting a limited war:

> The heart of the matter was the unwillingness of the American Government — and indeed the American people—to acknowledge or even comprehend the full implications of limited war. . . . Neither Congress nor the American people could, it was assumed, be persuaded to accept even limited losses of manpower or resources unless they believed that the stakes at issue were vital to America's security.

Instead of arriving at the most plausible conclusion, that a democracy should not fight such wars, Ball comes to the reverse conclusion, that such wars will probably be escalated.

> Since [accepting losses] was not possible if all we faced was a Communist takeover of such unimportant real estate as South Vietnam, there was a strong compulsion to recast our dilemma in terms that would justify something approaching total-war sacrifices. . . . The central question raised by this experience is whether a democratic state such as America can fight a limited war without serious danger of escalation toward a wider conflict.

But wars are not escalated in order to make them worthy of large sacrifices. Wars are escalated or extended or prolonged because they cannot be won at the existing level or scope of violence or within the calculated period of time. And in making the decision to escalate, the whole value of the original stake, in relation to the whole cost of the effort—the so-called "zero-base" calculus—is usually slighted. More salient at such a juncture is the calculation that the additional, or marginal, increment—whether of numbers, force, technique, scope, or simply duration—will be efficacious and that the additional costs and risks will at least be manageable. To raise at this point—as Ball and the proportionalists would do—the comparison of total stakes and total costs is either (1) to accept an adverse outcome and write off the entire investment or (2) to postulate the existence of some satisfactory third solution between winning and losing—some "political solution" (a postulation that, indeed, Ball made in his notable dissent of October 5, 1964[4])—with the implication that this political solution is there for the taking and somehow has been blindly overlooked or negligently discarded. But, if this third solution is not available, the effect of the doctrine of proportion is merely to increase the likelihood of ultimate defeat after the expenditure of much effort. Proportionalism invites intervention, but frustrates it by imposing limits just at the critical point.

Townsend Hoopes (himself a proportionalist critic), in a shrewd analysis of Vietnam, stresses rather the asymmetry of the stakes for the contestants—a condition that is not unique to Vietnam and could apply in future confrontations:

> We failed to see that the realization of our ostensibly limited objectives in Vietnam required in fact the total frustration of the other side's aims, and thus might well involve a wholly open-ended commitment.[5]

The problem, however, for the doctrine of proportion is that, *ex ante*, it is difficult if not impossible to predict the outcome of an exercise of intervention, precisely because certain critical conditions, such as the tenacity of the other side, are not subject to our determination. Thus the costs—at every point until our involvement is sealed and our forces are practically inextricable—may seem entirely in line with our real, not exaggerated or fictitious, interests.

Indeed, when our adversary can control the degree of escalation, the doctrine of proportion almost guarantees the worst situation. It limits us to an effort just inferior to the point required for success, while allowing the adversary to make that point continually more remote. Stalemate at ever higher levels of escalation is almost a logical deduction from the proportionalist premises. An even more general observation can be made about most limited wars. Wars that are geographically contained can not necessarily be limited also in duration or in the means required to terminate them (aside, of course, from the unilateral withdrawal of one of the contestants). Thus the whole concept of limited war is exposed as equivocal, if not paradoxical. In the case of Vietnam, war was unlimited as long as it was kept limited, and it could be limited only if it was made unlimited.[6]

The practical dilemma of all limited wars—how to win without indefinite escalation—leads a proportionalist to the elusive problem of how to quit if not winning. It is not surprising that George Ball turns to the question of "minimiz[ing] the costs of extrication." We could have extricated ourselves from Vietnam, he suggests, if an American president had defined and limited our commitment to "a promise that we would use our 'best efforts' to help the South Vietnamese help themselves. . . . There had to be a testing time —with the implication, of course, that if the South Vietnamese should fail the test it would be their fault, not ours." Unfortunately, this is spoken more like a lawyer than a strategist. It rather lightly characterizes the American stake (whether or not that stake was real or only imagined). The question is not the formality of whose fault it is if we are not succeeding in our common objective. The question is one of substance: if we are losing, but we still care about the outcome, what should we do?

What we lacked in Vietnam was not the wit to find a smooth and diplomatic way out. Probably none was available, neither the other side nor our own ally being willing to accord us any. Extrication, after the unwisdom of entry, would always have been a tough decision, with bad withdrawal symptoms and bad aftereffects. The choices were always more stark than the proportionalists were willing to admit.

The proportionalists fail to generalize broadly enough from our historical experience to formulate a presumption against intervention that will restrain future decisions where initially the odds look good and the effort looks reasonable. The lesson is not how to extricate—with honor or otherwise— but how not to intervene in the first place.

CHAPTER 7

The Economic Argument: Consequences and "Priorities"

Another group of critics has been hostile to the American posture toward Vietnam, and toward the Cold War in general, because of the consequences—the distortions of our economy and society, particularly the burgeoning of the military-industrial complex. These critics can be called *consequentialists*. They decry the pathology in American life resulting from thirty years of global intervention. They also deplore the high "opportunity costs" of defense preparations—the many items of social overhead, consumer preference, or private investment that could have been bought with the resources diverted to national security. Many of these consequentialist critics are professionals (economists, sociologists, political scientists), but the group also includes some perceptive legislative politicians.[1] Their watchword, which became ubiquitous as a popular rallying point, is *priorities*.

The consequential critique is a prevalent and a powerful

85

one; but, by itself, it is deficient.[2] There are two reasons for this judgment. The first is that the costs and the social distortions, severe as they may be, may not be a sufficient reason to curtail our defense efforts; and further, curtailing our defense efforts is not sufficient in itself to make our foreign policy more rational and benign. Since the consequential critique centers on the quality of domestic life, it could be neutralized by a different way of structuring and applying American force (for example, the Nixon Doctrine), which might have a reduced impact on our domestic system. Thus, unlike the fundamentalists, the consequentialists' concern is not particularly a moral one. Consequentialism could lend itself to reordering material allocations without much effect on the nature of America's role in the world. Priorities could mask the continuing exercise and enforcement of American privilege abroad, as long as it was cheap, successful, and domestically invisible, and as long as it contributed to the preferential enhancement of American life.

The second deficiency of the consequential critique is that it is not clear how—or even whether—savings in defense budgets translate into the enhancement of our domestic life. The consequential critique seems to be based on a mistaken model of the defense spending complex. The consequentialists assume that defense spending is related to domestic spending in a tight logical and fiscal framework, so that moderation of defense spending will lead to the automatic diversion of the savings to domestic needs.

No one actually claims that this will happen, but the model on which the consequentialists implicitly rely yields this hope, through (1) its basic assumption of scarce resources and (2) its concentration on the trade-off between the competing claims of the two areas, military and domestic. Of course, it is true that resources are scarce, in the sense that they are not free. And, of course, there is a sense—and there are even occasions—in which the decision-making system seems to accomplish this specific trade-off. This process occurs especially when expenditures are pressing upwards and domestic programs are curtailed as military costs rise. Even at these points, however, there are other possible ways in which the conflict of military and domestic claims can be accommodated—that is, if both the military and the domestic programs are considered to be worth maintaining. They include (1) a greater budget deficit (or a smaller surplus), or (2) higher taxes. The budget process does not always force hard choices. It does not in itself delimit the range of possible allocative decisions, much less determine the government's social philosophy or national security strategy.

When there are reductions in the military budget, however, the absence of an automatic connection between defense and domestic programs is more apparent. It is at least conceivable that military reductions will lead to a simple reduction in the federal budget rather than to reallocations.

These points can be made in a somewhat more technical way. The model implied by the consequential critique tends to make more ample domestic programs conditional on the reduction of defense spending, when they could more usefully be considered as independent elements. Why this is the case is indicated in the following analysis.

The analysis takes as its point of departure the classic statement of the consequentialist thesis and model in Bruce M. Russett's article, "Who Pays for Defense?"[3] Russett seeks to answer his question by deriving a series of historical relationships between defense spending and other subsectors of the gross national product. He presents a triangle of alternative allocations: (1) defense, or "guns," (2) private consumption, or "butter," and (3) private investment and government spending, or "structure." To simplify this discussion and sharpen the point, we can (a) drop out private investment[4] and (b) consider only those government expenditures in the field of health and education.[5]

The consequentialist model implies a symmetry of economic reactions to higher or lower levels of defense spending. This implication—critical to the consequentialist position

—misconceives the determinants of the allocative process. That is, the consequentialist model, though it records the strength of the correlations and the magnitude of the effects, ignores the whole process of decision making that mediates between the constraints (the limits of the economic, social, and political systems) and the allocations finally made. The independent variable (defense spending) and the dependent variables (private consumption and government expenditures) are simply the outside terms of a long and complex process; however impressively they may co-vary, they are not immediately related, causally. The independent variable itself (increased or decreased defense spending) may comprise, and thus conceal, several autonomous factors that come together in the budgetary decision process and may cancel or reinforce each other. These factors can interact in different ways to produce the same net, aggregate defense spending level and yet have very different implications for the dependent economic variable (the other sectors of the economy) and for noneconomic variables (types of force structures, weapons systems, strategic doctrines, and foreign policy responses). For these reasons the model of the consequentialists may not yield reliable predictions or good prescriptions.

The result of this blindness to the institutional structure of the system and the nature of its incentives is that the consequentialist model does not distinguish between the two manifestations of constraints. A constraint will "feel" different, and consequently have a different effect on behavior, depending on whether it is being approached as a limit on increasing activity or is being backed away from by decreasing activity. It matters whether decision makers are responding to feedbacks from the model indicating stringency or slack in the system (in the parlance of the system analysts, whether they are "pulling or pushing on a string").[6] When defense spending is to be increased, the consequentialist model treats constraints, realistically, as limits or trade-offs that must be respected by policy makers trying to fund the increased defense spending and allocate the costs or sacrifices. Here, the assumption of scarcity—that the economy is operating with little slack, forcing political trade-offs —is useful; at some point limits will be reached. The choices then will be (1) accepting inflation,[7] (2) levying higher taxes (which in turn cuts private consumption and private investment), or (3) cutting nondefense programs.

But when defense spending is to be decreased, the consequentialist model is misleading. This is the case of distributing the so-called dividend that should accrue from a decision to wind down a war. This decision may arise outside the consequentialist model, which is, after all, a narrow economic model; it may be prior to and independent of any observation of economic situations or consideration of economic effects. The consequentialists nevertheless assume a tight economy with full employment of resources and thus create the illusion that allocative trade-offs are actually forced and not just theoretically described.

The problem is two-fold. First, the economic model of the consequentialists does not explain why, or how, or toward what end, the decisions were made. In 1969, for example, a decision was made to scale down the war and decrease defense spending. This decision was made partially within the economic model, on the grounds that war costs (almost $30 billion out of a $79 billion annual defense budget) were starving other sectors and contributing to inflation, but also partially outside the economic model, on the grounds that the country was resisting the war.

Second, the fiscal dividend created by scaling down a war would be, at best, merely available for other uses. In fact, before the Vietnam dividend was even declared, it was partially preempted by other defense expenditures. In addition, the dividend was partially aborted through demand-reducing economic strategies designed to counter war-stimulated inflation—the course taken by the Nixon administration in its first economic game plan. (This is another possibility that the consequentialist model suppresses, in its assump-

tion of full use of resources.) So the decision to declare a
dividend (whether to private consumption, or private investment, or government civil expenditures) is not determined but only described by the model. That decision, like
the decision to reduce defense spending in the first place,
can be independent of the consequentialists' economic
model; that is, it can be determined by factors outside of
the economic model.

This is why it is not surprising that the consequentialists
fail to sustain the empirical case that cuts in defense spending will directly and commensurately benefit the public
civil sector (health and education).[8] Their model and their
demonstration are capable of supporting only the limited
assertion that defense cuts *could* result in benefits to the
public domestic sector—something that everyone knows in
the first place. The historical data do suggest that the dividend has more readily accrued to private consumption (particularly of consumer durables, presuming that the country
has the capital base to produce the increased amount) and
to some extent to private investment. The model in itself
does not tell why this has been the case, and thus it does not
indicate whether it would be the case in the future.

The point is this: Perhaps, as the consequentialists argue,
aggregate defense spending should be lower; perhaps aggregate domestic spending should be increased. But this is
not the whole of the matter: (A) Specific programs and noneconomic initiatives may also be needed. (B) Decisions on
defense spending and on domestic programs are independent of each other, especially when defense spending is
being reduced; independent decisions must be made (1) to
reduce defense spending and (2) to shape the alternative
allocations, through further separate decisions on (a) taxes
and budget deficits or surpluses and (b) specific government programs. (C) The allocation of the dividend from decreased defense spending is an object of competition—not
least by the military itself—to "resorb" the dividend before
it is even declared.[9] (D) The essence of this competition is

political rather than economic—though economic behavior provides some inputs into a larger political model, just as politics provides some inputs into an economic model. (E) Models that purport to explain the policy process should include and make visible these interesting features of choice. And (F) logically we should not make the defense cuts just because of the domestic priorities; and we should certainly not make the adjustments in our national security posture only if the proceeds are diverted to domestic uses.

Thus, the consequential critique, implying a grand and automatic trade-off between military and domestic expenditures, provides too indirect, aggregate, and neutral an approach to the motives and objects of defense spending. It is a useful critique but, in the last analysis, a partial one. It challenges inflated national security postures, but not for the ultimate reasons.

CHAPTER 8

The Fundamentalists: Morality
And Institutional Change

The fundamental critique of American foreign policy has two themes: immorality and institutional necessity. In both respects, fundamentalist critics, unlike the others, can view American foreign policy with the perspective—and perhaps the objectivity—that comes from renouncing allegiance to the "national interest."

The fundamentalists are struck, in reading the lessons of the other critics, by how much these lessons are really apologies. They function in the only way that apologies can be credibly presented by such critics: by fastening on the means, or the limits, or the domestic consequences of American policy without calling into question the validity of the national interest. Fundamentalists sense that the common denominator of the other positions is that American interests are validly defensible anywhere in the world, even in spite of the more natural interests of the people who exist and subsist there, so long as the means are effective or proportional or domestically tolerable. They fear that, once the validity of U. S. interests abroad is granted, the question of intervention becomes only a matter of style: the threshold, intensity, and persistence; the manipulation of proxies, counterpoint of diplomacy, finesse of threats and bluffs, reliance on legal form, and subjection to public rationalization. The fundamentalists contend that destructive intervention is immoral—not warranted on any grounds, even if successful, limited, and cheap.

Criticism in Depth

Often remarked during the buildup of intervention in Vietnam was the dearth of loyal antagonists within the administration or at least within the establishment—respected voices that might have swayed the decisions of the United States. But how can we expect to have found such voices within the foreign policy making community? The hallmark of loyalty—and therefore of respectability and even credibility—was conformity to the main conception of American interests. As long as the proposed measures of intervention promised to implement these interests successfully, there could have been no credible internal opposition.

The fundamental opposition had been exiled early and was to be found only among those, of suspect motives, whose vision of the world role and domestic character of the United States was out of accord with the standard definitions of the national interest. One is reminded of the Old Testament prophets, who confronted established policies on grounds that defied the very concept of the interest of the state, who tried to repair the bifurcated moral standard of the statesmen by insisting that the actions of human collectives such as governments and the actions of individuals must be submitted to a common judgment.

The second theme of the fundamental critique, institutional necessity, is also a thrust at the integrity of the national interest. The fundamentalists dare to ask "*whose* interests?" They see the asserted goals of the American system as particular objectives of its ruling circles and particular requirements of its current economic structures. As the Kolkos put it, "It is the expansive interests of American capitalism as an economy with specific structural needs that guide the definition of foreign economic policy and the United States' larger global role and needs."[1] That is the basis of the fundamentalists' assertion that the American system demands the suppression of foreign revolution (that is, any truly radical movement or program) and the control and compromise of the ostensibly sovereign states within the American orbit. The fundamentalists, like the proportionalists and the consequentialists, attack excessive military spending, but they insist that the defense budget is not the primary target. Focusing on it could be a diversion from the real problem and criticism of it too easily met with superficial and irrelevant remedies. The answer will not be found, they sense, until the American government understands revolution, not to subvert or subordinate it, but to tolerate it. Indeed, they feel that America should "make the world safe for revolution."[2]

We have seen, in an earlier discussion of the fundamentalist doctrine,[3] how the moral theme and the economic-institutional theme can clash, logically. The two themes are somewhat reconciled in the assertion that immoral and destructive interventions spring from the illegitimate, but real, objectives and requirements of a repressive class structure. But this assertion itself reveals a further tension within the fundamentalist position: the very hope that a country like the United States, retaining more or less the same basic social structure, could bring itself to tolerate revolution anywhere in the world is a contradiction in the eyes of the more severe and consistent neo-Marxist fundamentalists. One can distinguish—even among those who accept the fundamentalist argument that destructive intervention proceeds not only accidentally from immorality but in a more determined way from the very institutions of a capitalist society—two variants of this tenet. One view holds that intervention is merely perceived as a necessity by those who rule such a system (this, roughly, is the view of William Appleman Williams and Richard Barnet); therefore intervention might be an indicated, but not an inevitable and unalterable, output of the system. It is possible to imagine that the system can be damaged by holding and implementing interventionist attitudes and that therefore the system, and those who rule it, may be induced to change. This, in short, is a doctrine of reform. The other view holds that intervention is a real objective necessity of the capitalist system (this, roughly, is the view of Gabriel Kolko, Paul Baran, Paul Sweezy, and David Horowitz); therefore intervention is an inescapable output. Moreover, those who run the system are aware of the functionality of intervention, particularly in the third world, and it would be a logical and practical contradiction to expect them to change the system from within by self-induced reforms. (In this respect, the strict fundamental critique is the very opposite of the consequential critique, which asserts the disfunctionality of intervention, or certain kinds of intervention—its ruinous effect on our economy and social structure.) Nothing short of a complete social revolution, imposed by another class, can change the essential social and institutional structure, and thus the characteristic foreign policy outputs, of the system.

From the Fundamental Critique to the Strategic Remedy

The fundamental critique gives constructive attention to causal implications and systemic influences. It recognizes that effects do not proceed directly from wishes and that groups and nations respond in characteristic ways to objective conditions. The fundamentalists probe our attitudes and our system in depth—something that may not be true of other critics (instrumentalists, proportionalists, consequentialists), whose analysis may be causally shallow and therefore not effective in foreclosing undesirable future intervention.

The fundamentalists have the opposite probel: their analysis is too deep. It entails nothing less than a total change in the structure of institutions and the pattern of incentives in the domestic and international systems. On the institutional side, the fundamentalist critics ask: Why has intervention been attractive to certain American leading groups? Why, and how, have these groups promoted intervention? Their answers oscillate between automatic determinism and deliberate conspiracy. As we have seen, they themselves are somewhat ambivalent about how inevitable American intervention has been, or will be.

A more useful formulation would be: Why have American foreign policy elites responded by intervention to what they consider strategic challenge? The strategic critique, like the fundamental, recognizes the compulsions that arise from the way elites interpret external challenges; but the essence of the strategic critique is that it attributes the sense of the necessity of intervention rather to deep-seated presumptions about the shape of the world, the imminence of threats, and the political mandate to act on behalf of the nation. These factors are the ultimate determinants of the propensity to intervene—and they are strategic determinants.

The strategic critique thus postulates that almost any kind of foreign policy making group, operating through almost any conceivable institutions—but without "strategic" change —may feel compelled to make the same basic decisions as those that are criticized by the fundamentalists; whereas quite diverse foreign policy making groups, operating through a wide variety of institutional arrangements, including the present ones—but with a sharp change in presumptions about strategic requisites—could have a more constructive and more restricted set of orientations and reactions to events in the international system.

On the moral side of the argument, the fundamentalists would change the whole pattern of incentives that underlies the international system—the gravitational field that warps participant nations into destructive modes of statecraft, the pattern that statesmen in turn perpetuate as they attempt to derive power and advantage for their nations by exploiting some feature of the system. The solution required by the fundamental critique is that, in calculating costs, risks, and benefits, national leaders must consider, not narrow national advantage, but rather (1) the effects of a proposed act on the condition of their own—and other nations'—real constituents: individuals as the only repositories of affect, households as economic entities, and tangible and intellectual property as the capital base for generating values; and (2) the effects of the proposed action on the future propensities and motivational patterns of the entire international system.

The moral requisites of the fundamentalists are attractive. They are not necessarily utopian (though they may be improbable). But even one who sympathizes with the moral position of the fundamentalists must realize that it neglects the political-military consequences of the rigid and complete nonintervention that it implies. Two problems arise, which are interrelated. First, there must be some minimum strategic requisites—a baseline for any nation's foreign policy outputs—generated by the very notion of a responsible national government that can take moral positions and exercise restraint. These strategic requisites might sometimes cut across the ability of a state to abstain from exercises of force to preserve its security. Second, there must be some realization that the international system inhibits—or even penalizes—the unilateral exercise of moral restraint by an individual nation. The kind of world in which a state is situated affects the limits of its indulgence in moral foreign policies. These two problems are nothing but expressions of the situation of the nation-state in an international society of nation-states.

Thus, the difference between a fundamental and a strategic critique turns on whether intervention is seen as an institutional or a strategic necessity (and whether intervention is seen as a moral or a strategic fact), and consequently whether a policy of nonintervention requires a thoroughgoing change of institutions and moral values or a different set of strategic presumptions. The strategic critique senses that institutional change simply will not happen, and that even the moral regeneration of leaders is unlikely. It postulates that institutional change is unnecessary to curtail interventionist policies, and that moral regeneration is insufficient to achieve a change in national strategy, and indeed could leave a nation badly protected unless there were also a change in strategy.

The critical question for the fundamentalist position is: What if these moral and institutional changes cannot be accomplished, at home or in the world? In that case, the fundamentalists' question must be turned around. (1) If domestic institutional change is improbable, if we are still going to have a policy-forming elite and a people divided on basic social, economic, and political values, what kind of change will commend itself to such a nation? And (2) if the benign transformation of the international system is improbable, if we are going to have a quasi-anarchic world populated by autonomous and divergent nation-states, often irresponsible, destructive, or hostile, under what conditions will intervention be escapable?

So the issue becomes: How—in what kind of international system—can a nation afford the moral position of the fundamentalists? And how—under what set of presumptions—can a nation consistently carry out a noninterventionist policy?

When the moral and institutional critique of the fundamentalists is seen in this way, it leads to a strategic critique, and it invites us to draw strategic lessons from the situation of the United States in the world after its emergence from the shadow of Vietnam.

The Ultimate
Strategic Lessons

The strategic critique reads the lessons of America's foreign policy in the largest relevant way. It does not attempt to isolate or explain away experiences such as Vietnam (as would the proportionalists); or to mine them for small instrumental fixes; or to recast our efforts (as the consequentialists imply) to relieve some of the strains on our own system; or to condemn American conduct in itself or indicate social remedies that might overshoot the mark (as the fundamentalists tend to do). Rather, the strategic critique proposes that we derive the most general structural conclusions from our national experiences and make the most thorough changes in our actual dispositions to future challenges.

What we think we have learned from experience and how a nation (as a complex decision-making system) absorbs its experience are closely related. "Lessons" consist of what we are likely to do as much as what we ought to do. In fact, the predictive and prescriptive lessons bear on each

99

other: what we are likely to do influences and circumscribes what we think we ought to do; and what we think we ought to do partially determines and constrains what we are likely to do. The choices we actually make now often create the processes (instruments, institutions, doctrines, attitudes, and other existential facts) that will shape the choices we think we ought to make in the future. And the choices we think we ought to make in the future (influenced by rules and norms that will be observed) already constrain and inhibit the types of institutions (including armed forces and the manner in which we plan to use them) that we construct in the present.

The strategic critique captures this dual sense of prescription and prediction. The very notion of strategy—especially at the national level—implies choice within constraints. In this respect, strategy is somewhat like policy.[1] *Policy* can be defined as the orientation of a nation to future contingent choice within the constraints that will probably pertain. More theoretically, the structure of policy choice is bounded and shaped by the constraints of the policy process. The structure of choice reflects the alternatives that are objectively available, their trains of consequences, and their possible contradictions; it also reflects our basic strategic presumptions. The latter are the deep cognitive categories that condition our orientation to future strategic challenges, the ultimate criteria by which we choose the objects of our foreign policy and define the requisites of national security. The policy process represents the instruments, institutions, concrete dispositions, and attitudes embedded in our nation as a decision-making system. These function largely as constraints.[2]

I have said that learning a lesson from something means impressing upon oneself—one's way of structuring choices or one's decision-making process—a set of decision rules.[3] In the case of a significant experience such as Vietnam, that is emblematic of a more general state of affairs, such decision rules may amount to a broad, comprehensive alternative strategy that would dispose our system to respond to future challenges in categorically different ways. Decision rules are sets of *if-then* hypotheses, such that, if a certain state of affairs, or action of another party, or feature of a situation occurs or presents itself, then one will (prediction) or should (prescription) act in a certain way. But this programming of the decision-making process also presumes a way of analyzing situations that may be experienced. That is, a scheme must be constructed and imparted to, or embedded in, the intelligence apparatus of one's system that causes it to analyze situations in terms of those features that will trigger the appropriate decision rules. Thus, another important aspect of learning a lesson is to have a correct appreciation of the structure of situations, especially the structural similarities or analogies between events in our experience and events that might be experienced in the future.

The strategic critique, then, embodies both (1) a sense of the structure of choice—including an appreciation of the essential features of a historical situation that contributed to its outcome and that might pertain to future situations—and (2) a set of derived decision rules—both prescriptions and more concrete dispositions of the decision making system—that will apply to future situations in such a way that "better" outcomes will be attained.

With this theoretical sense of what the strategic critique would change and how it would change it, we should be clearer about the relation of the strategic critique to the position of the fundamentalists. The strategic and the fundamental views are not utterly antagonistic. The strategic approach would realize the moral goals of the fundamentalists, not directly by doing good and pursuing the good, but rather by structuring our own system and placing our system in circumstances such that the occasions for harm and damage are limited. The strategic approach, like the fundamental, would change the framework for policy choice extensively and deeply; but the categories of change would

not necessarily be, or be limited to, the economic and social
system.

The Presumption of Nonintervention

In considering national strategy, there is a classic progres-
sion of questions: (1) What are, or should be, our interests in
the world? (2) What kinds of wars should we fight; and
where, and on what grounds, should we impose limits on
intervention? (3) What forces, in number and kind, should
we maintain, and to what contingencies should they be
oriented? (4) How should we organize and manage our
military establishment most effectively for these missions,
and what should be the size and composition of the defense
budget?

The last two questions—the force structure, and the defense budget—are technical and specific. A strategic view
does not necessarily have direct and precise consequences
for force structures and defense budgets. Given a set of
worldwide objectives and possible contingencies, it is possible to evolve various force structures and defense budgets.
In general, they derive from the larger strategic orientations
and dispositions; but, in detail, they depend on certain
interior trade-offs among means, which are matters of efficiency or even bureaucratic bargaining among the military
services. There is a range of detailed solutions to the problem of means, within which one could be reasonably neutral.

The first two strategic questions—American interests and
the kinds of wars we should fight—are more philosophical
and less technical. And they have a good deal to do with
our whole national orientation to limited war. If we had to
make a large-scale projection of the probability and feasibility of limited war, we would encounter a certain contradiction. On the one hand, a prognosis for the entire international system is that it will be more prone to limited war—
probably in absolute terms and certainly in relation to the
incidence of general war. More limited wars are likely because of incursions of one nation into another, attempts at

forcible unification, irredentism over territories and populations, blackmail involving resources, and probing by major
adversaries through proxies at the fringes of their spheres.
And the world will be relatively more prone to limited war
than to general war because of the special inhibitions on the
principal nuclear powers.

On the other hand, it seems less likely that the United
States will be able to indulge—at least successfully—in exercises of limited war. This is because of constraints, mostly
domestic, that will inhibit the prosecution of nonessential
wars—"wars for no reason," balance of power wars—against
determined or irresponsible opponents. This judgment may
recall that of George Ball;[4] but our conclusions are quite
different. (1) Ball wants to reaffirm the necessity of, and preserve the will and capacity for, limited wars. (2) He sees the
case of Vietnam as prejudicing this objective because we
have tended to generalize falsely from its unique disadvan-
tages. (3) He fears that the American character will tempt
our leaders to present limited wars as total crusades in order
to justify our sacrifices. Thus, (4) he counsels that we ought
to learn, as a nation, how to fight limited wars for limited
objectives. In contrast, (1) the strategic critique takes Vietnam as an exemplar of a set of constraints—concrete, tangible, attitudinal—on the ability of the United States to
undertake limited wars. (2) It also sees Vietnam as an instance of a more general category of intervention; rather
than restricting the lesson of Vietnam, we should broaden
it into a strategic presumption against intervention. And
(3) it says that we should learn, not how to extricate ourselves from limited wars if things do not go according to
expectations, but rather how not to fight them at all.

On balance, we should avoid conflict ourselves in a world
that will continue to be limited-war prone, even if the world
thereby becomes somewhat more anarchic.

At first glance, the notion of a general presumption
against intervention raises some troublesome questions.[5]
Is intervention indivisible? Once we intervene in any degree,

is the damage done? Once we get beyond some threshold, can we discriminate among degrees? Is there any obvious way or place to stop, until the collapse of the other side?

But it is not necessary to accept these implications. Rather, the strategic critique suggests two more subtle propositions. (1) We can stop along the scale of escalation; indeed, constrained by circumstances, we will probably have to stop short of "winning." (2) Moreover, we are likely to self-impose a limit, which will only increase the chance of failing to win within that limit. It is for that reason that we should not intervene in the first place.

"The American Way of War"

The most important strategic lesson of the Vietnam War is that there are constraints that limit the production and projection of American military power. All the various types of critics recognize constraints of some kind. Some emphasize external, situational constraints; others emphasize internal, particularly economic, constraints.

What distinguishes the critics is what they would do about the constraints. Some instrumentalists—the military—analyzed the micro-mistakes and learned the mini-lessons: that a stubborn, unorthodox enemy might have to be countered, isolated, fixed, and destroyed by some unprecedented weapons and tactics. The liberal critics—generally proportionalists —concluded that the inhibiting and defeating features of Vietnam were quite special to this situation.

The conventional wisdom (instrumentalism as the prevailing official interpretation, proportionalism as the prevailing critique of the loyal opposition) seems to have converged on a four-part proposition. (1) The United States lost the Vietnam War (2) because of certain mistakes; (3) but we could do it over again, in another context, and (4) we should do it better next time.

The strategic critique suggests that this amalgamated wisdom is wrong on all four counts. (1) The United States gained some objectives in the Vietnam War; (2) mistakes were made, but it was not the mistakes that were decisive, and intervention and escalation were quite understandable choices; (3) we should never again do anything remotely similar, however, because (4) we cannot expect to improve either the conditions or our performance. Let us elaborate these points.

First of all, the United States achieved some of its goals in the Vietnam War—particularly after Nixon and Kissinger had redefined and reduced the goals, settling for a temporary stalemate, and had applied the shock and the weight of the means that the United States had in its arsenal to a target that suited these means.

Second, there were not critical mistakes in any of the senses of the word: things that we should have recognized but did not; or that, if recognized, would have produced different decisions; or that, if rectified, would have made a crucial difference in the outcome; or that we could have rectified even if we knew we had to.

Third, though there were not mistakes in the ordinary sense of the word, the choice that was made was no less disastrous. We should not have done it; and we should not hope or prepare to do it again in the future, in a wide range of situations, even situations that do not look like "Vietnams."

Fourth, the most elusive, but the controlling point: we cannot "do better" in the future. We cannot reconcile the peculiar capabilities and constraints of our political-social-economic system to the features of probable future situations. This has several implications.

One is that we will always make about the same quantity of mistakes, more or less—though they will differ in detail. Some particular mistake might be identified and some specific remedy invented, but we will never reduce the aggregate level of mistakes in some future situation, especially a dissimilar one. In short, it is unproductive to think of mistakes as a variable—especially as a manipulable or controllable policy variable. In the aggregate, at least, mistakes are not a variable at all; they are virtually a systemic constant, a parameter of our performance.

Another fact is "the American way of war."[6] It arises from the conditions of our society, polity, and economy. It is capital intensive, attaching a high value to the trade-off of American dollars against American lives. It does not directly engage all of the threats that we might experience; and it is annihilatingly destructive where it is applied. One conclusion is that it is simply beyond—or, more properly, beneath—the capabilities and the nature of our system to fight an "un-American" kind of war, such as Vietnam.

Conversely, what is within our capabilities—what grows out of our peculiar character as a nation—is irrelevant to many situations we may be called upon to remedy. It is a fact with profound moral as well as practical implications that we cannot wage the kind of war that even our allies would have us wage on their supposed behalf.

So both the quantity of mistakes and the quality of the American response are constants. They represent another kind of parameter or constraint on our ability to confront strategic challenge.

The trouble is not that we have failed to recognize the constraints. Even the Nixon Doctrine—and certainly the strategy of Nixon and Kissinger—were acknowledgments of and partial responses to the constraints. The trouble is that the instrumentalists, to some extent the proportionalists, and even the consequentialists still dream of overcoming the constraints, manipulating the parameters, changing the rules of the game, buying another chance, preparing for next time—in short, doing better.

But calls for renovating or restructuring our forces, weapons, or doctrines are to no avail. We can't, as a society, produce and project military forces or efforts much different from what we have done. The lesson we should draw from this is just the opposite of that perceived by the instrumentalist critics. We should scrutinize our performance and our nonperformance in Vietnam, not to determine how we can do better but precisely to see why we can't do better in the future. And we should take care to *over*learn this lesson so we will steer clear of any situation, generically—however compelling its particular circumstances might seem—in which we might be called upon to do much the same things.

The alternative—the strategic approach—is to live within the constraints, adjust to them, accept the consequences, hedge against the worst effects—but not plan to do the same things again. Of course, this is a very general prescription, but it has policy content. Specific situational prescriptions can be derived from it, and they will look very different from the prescriptions that are being distilled and purveyed by others—by the instrumentalists, the proportionalists, the consequentialists, the fundamentalists.

The international political-military "terms of trade" are tilting against the feasibility of intervention, against the presumption of limited war, against the discriminating, coercive, selective use of force. Each future replay will be more difficult, more elusive, more costly, more disastrous for our society and political system. With the present distillation of conventional wisdom, we might well become involved but find that we could not prevail or that we must exceed prudent or civilized bounds to shoot our way out.

Perhaps circumstances will eventually teach us the lesson that we must adjust to situations and outcomes rather than intervene to preempt or forestall them. Thus, putting more time and distance between ourselves and the experience of Vietnam, we may yet find ourselves more ready to forgive the micro-mistakes that might have been made but to give a wide berth to situations that seem to invite—even to justify— American intervention. But it would be better to learn this macro-lesson before, not after—and especially not during— the next round.

A General Prescription

The lessons to be learned from our foreign policy failures are not limited to a list of instrumental quick-fixes. That is, the lessons do not consist merely of some revised—even drastically reduced—force structure. Such revisions and reductions can be made for a variety of divergent reasons. They can be responses to economic or political constraints (the Nixon Doctrine); they can be the results of tight management, or shrewd fiscal measures, or technological trade-offs, or sharp changes in military doctrine.

Nor are the lessons exhausted by the limitations and escape mechanisms of the proportionalists. Nor are they contained in the consequentialists' statements of domestic priorities; there could be reductions in defense spending and increased efficiency in procurement, but we could still have policies that merely substitute cheap and cold destruction for expensive involvement.

Lessons are not even to be equated with the moral strictures of the fundamentalists, however powerful; for there must also be a strategic context that allows morality to be effective in governing our foreign policy.

The ultimate lessons of our international experience of the past several decades should be a set of strategic orientations, construed and applied with sufficient generality and consistency to have a constructive effect over the relevant range of future cases. The real lessons of history consist of these conceptual shifts in national strategy and profound changes in the categories through which we recognize events in the international system and interpret them as challenges to which we must respond.

Only the learning of such lessons will guard against a repetition of "Vietnams" in future—perhaps not recognizably similar—circumstances. But we must realize one thing: if we learn these strategic lessons, we will be purging ourselves of past failures such as Vietnam, but we will also be abjuring many other objects of our foreign policy.

PART IV

FUTURE CHOICES

CHAPTER 10

The Logic of the Domestic
and International Systems

The end game in Vietnam illustrates the several senses of the strategic lesson and reveals the peculiar logic of the domestic and international systems.

As the last outposts in Vietnam crumbled in March and April 1975, the administration castigated Congress for abandoning an ally, labeled certain Americans "isolationists," and predicted the worst consequences from our failure to stave off the collapse. Other Americans—hopeful politicians, wishful editorialists—denied the charges, rejected the epithets, and argued that Vietnam had little to do with the American position in the rest of the world, indeed, that release from Vietnam might benefit the American position elsewhere.

But, for several reasons, the fears expressed in the domino theory contained some truth. The reasons have to do with the process of American policy making, the reactions of allies and adversaries, and the resulting shape of the international system. These factors were sharply exemplified

111

and profoundly affected by the end game in Vietnam. And since they are not entirely subject to the control of American commentators or administrations, we cannot limit the damage of Vietnam to suit our hopes and consciences.

Before playing out the end game in spring 1975, we already knew that the powers of the Executive had been closely hedged about, since the Case-Church amendment, effective in August 1973, had prohibited reintervention in Southeast Asia. And perhaps we could have predicted the ultimate American default after Congress cut Vietnam appropriations, in 1974, from the administration's request of $1.4 billion to $700 million and failed to restore the cuts in winter 1975. Moreover, the trials of Watergate had run their course, with restrictive effects on the Executive license to make war. What happened confirmed the tendencies of the preceding year. Gerald Ford, a rather constitutional president (the first since Eisenhower, who had acted, or refused to act, similarly in the analogous Indochina crisis of April 1954), was content to put the decision on Vietnam and Cambodia up to Congress.

The consequences of our demonstrated failure to act may be more important than the consequences of the loss of Vietnam itself.

Damage Limiting

Most liberal and moderate observers reckoned that the loss of Vietnam was tolerable, even welcome; that intervention there had been a mistake; that we could choose, by an act of will and an expression of confidence, to limit the damage to American prestige, influence, and strategic position—and even enhance the value of these assets.

There were many comments to that effect. For example: "Reports of the imminent demise of American influence around the world, many of them emanating curiously from high administration officials, are clearly very premature."[1] "Past errors must not now be compounded by a misreading of their meaning for the future. This country's failure in

Indochina is, as President Ford has so succinctly stated, neither the end of the world nor the end of America's role in the world. . . . This country's tragic misadventure in Indochina in no way diminishes the need to keep and make international commitments."[2] "Henry Kissinger acted like a child with a wounded ego exaggerating his loss. 'Look how unreliable we are,' he told the world in effect. 'Look at the disaster our perfidy has caused.'"[3] ". . . [T]he basic fact is that the Vietnam experience is not powerfully relevant to the present problems of the United States."[4] "The sources of U. S. power are intact, despite Indochina."[5] And finally, "At least there was no need to make the end even worse by proclaiming what could be called a self-domino theory."[6]

Even the administration eventually joined in this interpretation.[7] In a major foreign policy speech to Congress on April 10, even while urgently requesting $722 million in aid for Vietnam, President Ford used the occasion to recite positions of American strength and to pledge renewed support of our commitments. For this, he was applauded by the *Washington Post*: "President Ford quietly banished the domino theory from presidential policy."[8] Later, in a speech on April 23 at Tulane University, Ford gave up the game of recriminations against Congress and joined his liberal critics in the exercise of damage-limiting: "[The events in Indochina] portend neither the end of the world nor of America's leadership in the world." Again, Ford was widely applauded. As the *New York Times* put it: "The end of the misguided military adventure in Indochina should make it easier to return to Lincoln's vision of the American destiny." A few weeks later, on the night of the final American evacuation from the roof of the embassy in Saigon, President Ford, in his own attempt at a Lincolnesque statement, said: "The time has come to look forward to an agenda for the future, to unify, to bind up the nation's wounds and to restore its health and optimistic self-confidence."

The entire American political center, anxious to avoid external humiliation and internal division, had embarked on the creation of a new myth: that Vietnam never really mattered; that it was a special case, an unnecessary one at that; that it was separable, or at least containable; that its loss might even be a blessing and a source of renewed strength—that America would be even steadier, more reliable, its assurances and guarantees more credible, now that we had shed this "irrational" and "aberrant" situation; that the United States could smoothly transform its military role into some other form of functional leadership—diplomatic, economic, or just spiritual. All we had to do was to cure our hubris, recognize the limits, even the nonexistence, of our interest in Southeast Asia; and then, presumably, our adversaries would stop challenging us; our friends would stop doubting our firm will, benevolent intention, and good sense; and our own people would renew their grant of trust in their government. In short, "no dominoes."

There were no recollections of earlier judgments, such as this typical one from the *New York Times* twelve years before (November 3, 1963): ". . . the loss of South Vietnam to the Communists could raise doubts around the globe about the value of U. S. commitments to defend nations against Communist pressure. . . . The impact on revolutionary movements throughout the world would be profound. At best, neutralism in the East-West struggle might spread. In much of Asia there might be a feeling that the Communists—under the leadership and inspiration of Peking—represented 'the wave of the future.'"

There were no apologies by President Ford or Secretary of State Kissinger for their earlier statements, predicting inescapable reactions of allies, adversaries, and the American people. Kissinger, when Assistant to the President, in a background briefing at San Clemente on June 26, 1970, had said: ". . . we certainly have to keep in mind that the Russians will judge us by the general purposefulness of our performance everywhere. . . . [W]hat we do in Vietnam has to be measured in terms larger than Vietnam itself, and history teaches us that people do not forgive their leaders for producing disasters, even if what they do seems to reflect their immediate wishes." And, in a news conference on March 26, 1975, as Secretary of State, Kissinger had said: "We must understand that peace is indivisible. The United States cannot pursue a policy of selective reliability. We cannot abandon friends in one part of the world without jeopardizing the security of friends everywhere. . . . [Though] we are not saying that every part of the world is strategically as important to the United States as any other part of the world, the problem we face in Indochina today is an elementary question of what kind of a people we are. . . . This is a fundamental question of how we are viewed by all other people, and it has nothing to do with the question of whether we should even have gotten involved there in the first place. . . . There is no question that events in Portugal, Greece, Turkey, and Indochina had an effect on the conduct of the [Middle East] negotiations. On the part of our friends, it raised the question of the durability of our assurances. And since one of our problems was to substitute American assurances for some physical terrain features, this was a factor." And President Ford, in a news conference at San Diego on April 3, 1975, had said: "I believe that in any case where the United States does not live up to its moral or treaty obligations, it can't help but have an adverse impact on other allies we have around the world."

The logic of these earlier statements was not false. Only the premises were untenable: that our position in Indochina, which was deemed necessary for America's global influence and control, could in fact be sustained, or that it was worth the cost in lives, resources, and destruction. It is true that harping on the dominoes, on the probable effects of American unreliability, can be a self-fulfilling prophecy. The trouble is that it has a basis in objective fact, in the independent actions of other parties that are not subject to our control. The corresponding trouble is that the opposite model—that of the liberal critics and later the administration pragmatists—is not even a self-fulfilling prophecy. It is a self-delusion, designed for domestic consumption, as a salve to our pride, an antidote to "recriminations." At worst, it could be a multiple disaster—for those allies who believe it and continue to depend on American assurances, and for us, if we are called upon in the future to redeem our reaffirmed expressions of support.

The stubborn latter-day hawks (and their mirror images, our domestic radicals) were always closer to the truth of the matter. Certainly they have been more faithful to their original analysis, which was once the shared wisdom of a wider spectrum of American opinion: Vietnam did matter; expressions of American will and intent in one part of the world, or a default or aborted effort by the United States, do have an impact on other areas and other relationships; they do affect the American position in the world, and consequently the shape of the international system. The question was always whether we should accept the challenge or accommodate the loss, with all its consequences. In any case, the liberal and moderate prognosis of the effects of the end game in Vietnam—the damage-limiting scenario—is just too good to be true.

Distractions

Some nonessential issues were avidly pursued, as a distraction from the underlying structural lessons that were there to be learned. One such issue—perhaps the most salient in the waning hours of the war—was the concern that we honor our debts to those Vietnamese who had aided our cause. There was much concern over the treatment of the refugees who reached our country.

Another distracting question was "Who was responsible for the loss?" Many took this to be the essential question— the one to be either settled or avoided if we were to escape the kind of recriminations that followed the fall of China to the Communists in 1949. Various propositions were advanced, none of them conclusive or comprehensive. One was that defeat was the narrow result of President Thieu's tactical incompetence—by some accounts, the result of a

single error by a single incompetent commander in the
highlands of the Second Corps area, who, by a disorderly
withdrawal, began the unraveling of Saigon's entire military position.[9] Other interpretations covered the rest of the
spectrum of possibilities: the general ineffectiveness of the
ARVN (Army of the Republic of Vietnam), its continuing
dependence on American assistance and methods; the un-
willingness of the South Vietnamese to fight, or their lack
of anything convincing to fight for; and—closer to home—the
failure of Congress to provide enough assistance, and the
inhibiting effects of the military cutoff of August 15, 1973, in
foreclosing the possibility of American reintervention or
retaliation to police the Paris accords of January 1973 with
North Vietnam.

A closely related issue was whether Thieu's regime ever
deserved our support; whether we should have, or could
have, used our leverage to exact his compliance with the
Paris accords; and whether this would have averted or postponed—or hastened—the demise of the Thieu government.
The implication of this kind of argument—not always intended—is that we might have salvaged something short of
abject defeat and that in future cases we might make even
greater use of American influence.

Another distracting non-point was that we had done
enough for South Vietnam, or the Saigon government, or
Thieu, and that they were ungrateful. Of course, "enough"
to satisfy our private criteria might not have been enough
to satisfy the objective demands of the situation.

The most weighty of the nonessential issues is whether
Vietnam was ever a real interest of the United States. The
contention that it was not is one of the props of the damage-
limiting argument. If Vietnam was never really an interest,
then all we need do is acknowledge our mistake and the
future will hold no terrors for us; indeed, it will present enhanced opportunities for an intellectually regenerated foreign policy. But this would achieve only absolution, not im-
munity, from the effects of the collapse in Vietnam.

A salient contention in the argument that Vietnam was of

little intrinsic interest for the United States is that our intervention was based on the misperception that communism
was "monolithic." It might well have been the case, as
Harold R. Isaacs pointed out,[10] that "Vietnamese communism was as nation-centered as Stalin's, Tito's and Mao's,
perhaps even more so." What this contention overlooks,
however, is that challenges to the situation of a great nation
never come in a single size and shape; but they may nevertheless be challenges. Future sources of disorder will be
variegated and not necessarily ideologically aligned or strategically concerted. There will be local revolutionary movements; willful nationalist states, including many that are
noncommunist; and opportunistic large powers. The very
heterogeneity of communism may make it more troublesome for the United States; local communists will be less
likely to be restrained by dictation from Moscow, which
may well want to preserve detente and a semblance of global
condominium.

The nonissue of nationalism, like the others, is the property of the pragmatic and liberal center. Neither the right
nor the left makes that particular case. Rather, right and
left alike make two valid points about recent American
interventions: (1) The question of whose interests are at stake
is not limited by the identity of the immediate contestants
in the conflict; nor is it a matter of the choice of the contestants. It is a wider and a more objective matter. Thus, it
does not make much difference (even if it is true) that the
communists in Vietnam represented a nationalist movement; and it does make a difference (whether some of us
wish to acknowledge it or not) if we lose and how we lose.
(2) Therefore, if we are unable to generate the requisite
means or adopt the requisite tactics to win such conflicts,
or if we cannot reconcile the necessary behavior with our
essential values, then we are confronted with a conclusion
that will not be as limited and painless as most liberals
think. We must give up a whole category of interventions.

What all these nonissues prove is that, if we ask the

wrong questions, we are likely to get the wrong answers. The questions are wrong because they are not operational questions about future American performance or about the reactions of other nations that, together, constitute the future international system in which American foreign policy will have to perform.

America the Unreliable?

The consequences of our recent experience as a nation are not containable by our will or desire since they result from (1) the operation of our own system and (2) the structure of the international system.

The first point is that the American performance in Vietnam revealed how our own polity, society, and economy work as a policy-making system. It particularly revealed the constraints that Congress and the people put on the actions of the Executive. The critical question is: How is our behavior likely to manifest itself in future situations, even those that are different in certain respects from Vietnam? After all, the future contingent reactions of a nation constitute its policy; and in turn the internal policy process of the nation defines the limits of American assurances and commitments, including the renewed assurances our leaders put about in the wake of Vietnam.

The trouble with the myth of damage limitation is precisely that it ignores the policy process. It does not take into account that policy is the product of complex systems, not of individual wills, and that these systems have restraining as well as motivating elements. The largest intentions, the most earnest attempts at credibility, and the highest honor of leaders may be severely impaired, and sometimes completely obstructed, by the operation of the entire political, social, and economic system.

Our peculiar constitutional system of countervailing powers is useful for the last-ditch protection of domestic liberties but frustrating to external adventures, cold-war constancy, or balance-of-power potency. (It was probably designed by the founders of this country to work precisely that way.) It was the internal constraints that the public and Congress put on the actions of the Executive—interacting, of course, with the constraints of the international system (the behavior of other nations, the diffusion of power)—that undid our position in Vietnam.

This proposition is resisted not only by American liberals but by many exponents of Asian democracy; for example: "The proposition . . . that Indochina has fallen to the communists because it was abandoned by the United States—is shrouded in . . . illusion. . . . Thieu and Lon Nol fell because they were abandoned by their own people. . . . It is a bitter piece of reality but it should be more comforting to Americans than the half-truth that Thieu and Lon Nol fell due only to the lack of American military support."[11] My point, however, is that indigenous popular support, though it was lacking, was neither a necessary nor a sufficient condition for the perpetuation of the regimes in Vietnam or Cambodia. The interdiction of American military intervention by our Congress remains the essential condition that enabled the fall of Saigon and Phnom Penh to the communists. It might be more accurate to say that Vietnam and Cambodia fell because the American government had lost the support of its people. And this is a fact that does have consequences for the reliability of American commitments in the future.

Externally, only those who do not understand the working of the total American foreign policy process can be reassured by the promises of our Executive Branch in the wake of Vietnam. It does not reinforce our commitments when the Secretary of Defense, Harold Brown, replies, "in a trembling voice," to an impertinent challenge by an Asian journalist in South Korea: "That the United States observes its commitments to other countries is nowhere shown more clearly than in the case of the Vietnam War."[12] What is at stake is not the will or fervor of a president or his advisers. What hobbled U. S. policy in Southeast Asia was not the reluctance of the Executive Branch to implement its commitments. It was the eventual resistance of Congress and the public to prolonging the sacrifice of lives and resources in situations that were not compelling or clear. Thus, it is not some "trauma" of Vietnam that will inhibit American responses in the future. It is the structural similarity of future challenges that will predictably evoke the same constraints on the projection of American power. The reliability of the American response was the first casualty of the end game in Vietnam.

The second point is that, in turn, the performance of the American system in the end game of Vietnam has had a tangible and profound effect on the actions of other countries, allies and adversaries, and is consequently changing the shape of the international system. Other nations cannot simply speculate about the future performance of the United States; they must do something about it. Nations that have depended on us and nations that have feared our response will, respectively, hedge against our default or probe our further reactions. Each nation will do this in its own way, according to its strategic situation. This is why "dominoes" are neither perfect as an analogy nor obvious as a fact; but it is also why they are nonetheless real.

There is such a thing as "dominoes," though they are not the crude mechanistic geographical dominoes—the fall of one contiguous country after another—that have been so derided. They are, rather, political and psychological. (This does not mean that they are subjective; they constitute objective elements in the system. One man's subjectivity is another man's objectivity; others' images are our facts.[13]) Nations that are geographically removed are affected, in no particular spatial sequence, as they draw conclusions about the constancy of American support and the integrity of their alliances or protective arrangements with the United States. The very structure of the international system has been affected by the way Vietnam ended, as much as by the war itself.

In the most general terms, the shape of the international system is determined by every country's expectation of the behavior of each important country. The international system is not a simple thing but a construct, a summation of the relationships among nations, that ultimately depends on two elements: (1) what countries can do to one another, and (2) what they intend to do to one another. The experience of Vietnam may have disillusioned some observers— and properly so—about the efficacy of military force; but this judgment does not change the fact that the shape and character of the international system depend, in the last resort, on the ability and propensity to use or threaten force to defend friends, strategic assets, and political values. We cannot discount these elements completely or conform them entirely to our predilections, since they are to a large extent independent of our will.

But the capabilities and intentions of nations are still inevitably affected by the operation of America's own decision-making system. More specifically, U. S. leadership in the world—during the thirty-year post–Second World War regime of the bipolar system and the subsequent brief reign of the balance of power—has rested on the high probability of our intervention, our capacity and resolve, relied on by others, to do something for our friends if they, or their systems or values, are threatened (or, in the balance of power system, to do something even for adversaries, such as China, for the sake of the stability of the system). Historically, that has been both the test of leadership and the essential condition for maintaining a particular kind of international system.

Thus, the conclusion of Vietnam has provided an early clue of the instability of the balance of power (even as it was installed by Nixon and Kissinger, at a more modest level of American effort and with a more pluralistic distribution of power and responsibility). The dilution of American guarantees makes it both more necessary and more feasible for allies, proxies, and friends to accommodate adversaries, or to strike a posture of neutrality, or to attempt more equidistance between the great powers, or to pursue self-reliance even to the point of acquiring a national nuclear force.

The point, again, is not simply that the United States defaulted in the end game of Vietnam, but that in generally similar (not necessarily identical) instances in the future it would be subject to the same kinds of constraints and therefore prone to the same patterns of behavior. The only prudent conclusion our allies could draw is that the United States is not a dependable ally. It does not matter that the United States may still remain "selectively" engaged in many parts of the globe or that it will undoubtedly retain the raw capacity for a potent response. It certainly does not matter that allies have been the objects of renewed pledges by American leaders. They would be foolish to depend to the same extent as before on American guarantees, if these were not redundant with alternative defense or diplomatic arrangements they had already made. Specifically, even less than before can nations, such as Israel, afford to exchange tangible strategic assets for American guarantees of future contingent support—even in the form of an explicit mutual security pact, let alone the personal assurances of a series of transient (in several senses) secretaries of state. They must hedge—now more widely than ever—against the possible failure of an American response. The dependence of allies on our commitments, and the efficacy of these commitments in stabilizing the international order, are the second casualty of the end game of Vietnam.

When the matter is put this way—in terms of structure, cause, and effect—it should be clear how little relevant are the accusations of "isolationism" (though it may be true that the innate, residual American attitude toward the world, which is now reasserting itself in a number of ways, is a kind of de facto noninterventionism). This facile abstraction not only misrepresents and oversimplifies the American attitude, but it puts the matter on the wrong ground. We are not talking about a subjective psychological phenomenon or

124   Future Choices

a preferred philosophy of international order. The issue is more tangible and more objective. It concerns the specific operations of the American policy-making system, including its constraining elements; and it concerns the actual reactions, the necessary hedges, of allies and the probable strategies of adversaries.

Strategic Ripples

The effects of the end game rippled out from Vietnam and Cambodia. There was the resuscitation of factional warfare in Laos, subverting the accords of 1973 and leading to the final collapse of the coalition regime. There were the feverish accommodations of Thailand to the concerns not only of China—an old story that dated from the Nixon Doctrine and the American approach to Peking—but also of Hanoi. The Thai foreign minister referred to the United States as a country that "does not have any morals at this point"—deriding the assurances of Secretary of Defense James Schlesinger; and the Prime Minister of Thailand ordered the 27,000 U. S. airmen withdrawn within a year and the five U. S.–used bases returned to Thai control.

The government of the Philippines had second thoughts about the two major U. S. bases on its territory, Clark Air Base and the naval installation at Subic Bay; and President Marcos challenged the Mutual Security Treaty with the United States. President Lee Kuan Yew of Singapore said: "[W]hat is happening [in South Vietnam and Cambodia] is having a profound effect on the minds of others in Southeast Asia, particularly Cambodia's immediate neighbors, the Thais." Lee saw the United States as "no longer [able to] intervene in Southeast Asia," and predicted a regional power contest "mainly between the People's Republic of China and the Soviet Union."[14] Taiwan alone professed to trust the American security guarantee, but began secretly to build a plant to reprocess nuclear fuel, possibly for the future production of weapons.[15]

South Korea intensified its worries about a North Korean

move for forcible reunification of the peninsula and ruminated about acquiring a national nuclear capability. The extended visit (April 18–26, 1975) of North Korean Premier Kim Il-sung to Peking might have been obscure in its intent, but it was not an accident. Japan, generally unnerved, sent its Foreign Minister to Washington in mid-April 1975 to seek a conspicuous pledge of support for the Security Treaty. And later, the Australian Prime Minister told the new Chinese Premier that the conflict between the American Congress and President was frustrating our ability to counter the expansion of Soviet influence, particularly in Southeast Asia.[16]

Farther afield, Israel expressed doubts about relying on American protection in return for making strategic concessions. Israel can always be moved somewhat by American pressure, because of its own lack of real alternatives; but it will try to hedge against a critical American default and to maintain its freedom of action for reprisals and preemption.[17]

In Europe, too, the American default in Vietnam had its indirect effect. Of course European leaders professed to dissociate Vietnam from their own circumstances. They do not relish having to make a public reassessment of the American connection, whatever its strains and cracks, since all alternatives are measurably worse. But even the American creation of three additional divisions, two of them oriented to the defense of NATO, as well as its improved ability to deploy troops to Europe and Senator Mansfield's forbearing, for the first time in eight years, to introduce his perennial resolution to cut forces in Europe, did not still the renewed fears of a "decoupling" of America's ultimate response from the fate of Europe.

A Mighty Fortress

There is yet another lesson that our allies must draw from Vietnam and from our manner of leaving it: that the United States will not defend allies as they prefer to be defended.

No doubt we will still intervene in some conflicts, particularly where we perceive the Soviets to be the real adversary or the major beneficiary. But the entire American mode of defense is not that of a steadily committed global imperial power, continuously maintaining its magnetic field of force over the whole strategic universe.

Geography and the circumstances of the founding and building of this nation have—for better or worse—endowed us with a fortress mentality. We give battle, if necessary and when provoked, but we fight unilaterally. We are likely to use leverage on an ally to secure certain reforms that will make our temporary alliance more palatable. We will pursue a war to an unconditional, sometimes unnecessary, outcome; or we will abandon the field when it suits our purposes—when we think we have done "enough." (President Thieu's parting complaint, though querulous and ungrateful, was, in this particular sense, quite accurate. After all, the United States had extricated itself from Vietnam by bargaining for its prisoners, coercing the enemy in a convincing but locally irrelevant way, fabricating an overhead deal with its ally's mortal adversary, signing a cosmetic and imperfect agreement on behalf of the local contestants, and forcing it down its ally's throat.)

In sum, our defensive efforts in the world are last-ditch, self-serving, overwhelming, destructive—and above all intermittent. Potential allies ought to be more wary about inviting the United States to rescue them from their troubles.

The experience and the outcome of Vietnam have further affected the options available to the United States in waging war. One of the effects of Vietnam was to cast a shadow on the feasibility of limited conventional war. During the late 1950s and early 1960s, limited war, graduated response, and counterinsurgency were invented to resolve the dilemma of holocaust-or-paralysis presented by the prospect of nuclear parity and nuclear plenty. Logically, limited war should be even more appropriate now, when nuclear parity and plenty have been amply realized. But the option of limited conventional war has been clouded by the experience of Vietnam. It is both significant and ironic that Vietnam ended by prejudicing limited war, for Vietnam was the paradigmatic case of limited war, both in its rationale and in its execution.

By the end of the first Nixon term, the American government had been led to the conclusion that intervention, if attempted, must be decisive and escalation dramatic. The way in which President Nixon ended the American phase of the war—with bombing and mining, bluster and threat—upset some previous judgments about what this war proved. Nixon's action might have, momentarily, resuscitated belief in the feasibility of military actions.[18] Indeed, if the culminating North Vietnamese offensive of 1975 had been indefinitely postponed and our learning had been limited to the earlier phase of Vietnam—the one that ended with the mining of Haiphong, the Christmas bombing of Hanoi, and the Paris accords of January 1973—we could have concluded that the decisive application of force and the threat of further escalation were *the lessons* of Vietnam. Now, America's likely courses of action include decisiveness or default—neither of which will satisfy the defensive preferences of our allies.

Vindication of the Best and the Brightest

The more seriously we construe the lessons of the end game in Vietnam, the more we implicitly vindicate the policy makers of the early and mid-1960s who responded to the challenge in Vietnam, and the administration of Nixon and Kissinger that sought to avoid obvious defeat. Those policy makers believed that Vietnam was a challenge of more than local or regional import, and one that we could not safely decline for more than domestic political reasons— for reasons that had to do with the nature of the international system and the continuity of American influence. To expect, now, that they might have viewed the challenge

differently, that they might have accepted the large risks
of default, is anachronistic. However these fateful decisions
turned out, they were not trivial or cynical, and they certainly were not the result of psychological aberration or
bureaucratic maneuver.

Those policy makers, throughout the 1960s and early
1970s, genuinely sensed that an American default in Vietnam would (1) undermine the credibility of America's global
guarantees, (2) hasten the advent of a future choice between
nuclear war and accommodation of our major adversaries,
and (3) precipitate, as Lyndon Johnson expressed it, "an
endless national debate—a mean and destructive debate—that
would shatter my presidency, kill my Administration, and
damage our democracy."[19] The very reaffirmations, after the
fall of Vietnam, of the continuing validity of our other security commitments, by the same people who had criticized the
Vietnam War, are back-handed acknowledgements of the
prospective consequences that had impelled earlier decision
makers to intervene and persevere in Vietnam.

If our international position is now compromised, and if
the collapse in Vietnam has hastened the evolution of the
international system out of our control, the policy makers
of the Kennedy-Johnson era and the Nixon-Kissinger ad-
minstration are vindicated—in a way, despite themselves. I
say "despite themselves" because, if their choice of intervention and escalation in Vietnam was indeed purposeful
and logical, not a mistake, and if this choice led to disaster,
then the same logic will lead to future encounters, some
just as disastrous—a conclusion they would be reluctant to
admit. In other words, to pronounce this vindication, one
need not accept the validity of the decisions to intervene
and escalate in Vietnam. One need only recognize the logic
of choice: they did what they did because they "had to" do
it (and therefore they would do it again). But there is a
warning here: to the extent that one repudiates these decisions (as I do), one must accept the train of consequences
that now follows from America's eventual default in Vietnam.

A Lethal Myth

Most statesmen and observers from the moderate and liberal center are unwilling to accept this train of consequences. They would have the United States remain strategically engaged with the world, but more selectively. They seek an active foreign policy for the United States, but with fewer risks and lower costs. They reaffirm commitments to "worthy" allies, but attempt to minimize the consequences of possible contingencies.

But this prescription is less a policy than a hope. It will not be up to the United States to select the next threat, the next challenge, the next contingency. The United States will not be able to trim its commitments artfully to fit the cloth of its capabilities—Walter Lippmann's classic admonition. Adversaries will not respect our defensive priorities. Allies will be wary of accepting the meticulously limited guarantees of a nation that cannot find the will or the purpose to extend them or honor them more generally.

In castigating what they consider the myopia of those who stubbornly chose to stand in Vietnam, the proponents of selectivity forget that wars must be taken as they come, with their intractable features, their uncertainties, and sometimes their long odds against convenient victory. If we cannot take wars as they come, then we must avoid them in wide moves of policy direction, long before they happen, and that means shedding commitments—by devolution, perhaps, but not by some neat tailoring. In the end, selectivity toward commitments is part of a larger syndrome that includes the myths that the damage of Vietnam can be limited and that Vietnam was a mistake and its lessons, if any, are dispensable.

The myths of a nation are functional: they are the half-truths and half-lies—the explanations we know are false and yet choose to believe—that gloss over divisions and bind a society together. It is painful, therefore, to challenge them.

But perhaps we should not rest so easily with the new myths of Vietnam. Though they made our exit from Vietnam more tolerable and politically safe, they are intended to salvage from the debacle of our ambitions and intentions in Vietnam the capacity and the will for future intervention. Of course, there is the hope that our renewed global leadership will be benign—humanitarian, economic, diplomatic—anything but "military." Indeed, the apologists for amnesia about Vietnam and renewal of the American global engagement would have it that the principal fault of our foreign policy, from Truman to Nixon, was its militarization.

Along with this call for a reassertion of American leadership in the world has come, not unnaturally, a call for a renaissance of presidential leadership at home. Saving only the ritual purification of the removal of Richard Nixon, many are already saying that the pendulum has swung too far toward congressional government, that we face immobilism or incoherence if the tendency goes unchecked.

So we must consider that there are two kinds of lethality. There is the *Lethe* of forgetfulness and renewal—the healing qualities of these myths about Vietnam, particularly the intention to avoid recriminations and enable this country to unite and get on with its business. But there is also the danger that, by obscuring the reasons and the lessons of our encounter in Vietnam—by evading the deep and wide conclusions we ought to draw and the fundamental changes in foreign policy that should follow from them—this country may invite the lethality of another encounter, perhaps in a place and in circumstances that do not look like the last one.

In short, we may have to risk either some recriminations or another Vietnam.

CHAPTER 11

Adjusting to a
Second-Best World

The collapse of the American effort in Vietnam was a punctuation, marking, but not entirely creating, a turning point in our national choices and in the possibilities of the international system.

For several years, the international system and American foreign policy have been at a turning point—or rather in the midst of an extended period of transition and choice—the first serious one since the post–Second World War sequence that led to the Truman Doctrine in 1947, the Korean War in 1950, and the commitment of American troops to Europe in 1951. Turning points are junctures where the international system has lost its previous organization and configuration, where a range of alternative states of the system is available, and where the decisions of major powers can be decisive in determining the shape of the system. Turning points are thus occasions for great debates. Over the past decade, we have been experiencing such a great debate about our basic foreign policy orientation—a debate partially precipitated and partially masked by the Vietnam war.

By the beginning of the 1970s, the international system had clearly evolved beyond the bipolarity of the previous two decades (though important elements of duality and a predominant axis of confrontation persist). An emerging multipolar balance of power was both recognized and codified by Nixon and Kissinger, partially in an attempt to compensate for the unraveling of Vietnam. From a neutral perspective, the pursuit of a more diversified global balance of power was a perceptive and intelligent response of the Nixon-Kissinger regime. It was an effort to relieve the constraints and resolve the contradictions of the previous policy and the preceding state of affairs. It was an attempt to preserve the essential American position in the world and also the essence of American control of the shape of the international system, but with less risk and more economy of means. But the balance of power approach contained and engendered contradictions of its own. In any event, it was never firmly or durably installed. It must now be regarded as transient.

Some large-scale alternatives have been suggested and have acquired considerable sponsorship. There is, for example, persistent sentiment for building, or rebuilding, authoritative supranational institutions. Some versions represent a return to the collective security that was attempted at the end of the Second World War; other versions entail the creation of a "managed interdependence." Some people have even envisioned the blossoming of detente into a sort of working condominium of the two superpowers.

There is also considerable advocacy of a reconstruction of alliances with politically compatible nations and a renewed infusion of traditional moral criteria into American foreign policy. This would represent a partial return to the conditions of bipolar confrontation. Elements of this approach, rhetorical and practical, are apparent in the program of President Carter and some of his foreign affairs advisors.[1]

The balance of power and the alternatives of global management and revived bipolar competition might be bracketed as mechanisms and schemes to perpetuate our international control. Opposed to all of these variants of managed worlds and strategies for American control would be a more loosely structured and less institutionalized world and a corresponding American policy of substantial political-military disengagement.

This alternative policy of disengagement is based on a certain set of expectations of the international system.

1. The ability of any single nation, or combination of nations, to control the international system is decreasing. This phenomenon can be termed a *diffusion of power*. It will have several aspects: (a) the fragmentation of centers of effective and coordinated power (such as alliances or regional groupings); (b) the impracticality of military force, whether nuclear, conventional, or subconventional; and (c) the intractability of sources of disorder and violent change to the application of political-military pressure. It is doubtful that power will be distributed in such a way as to be manageable in itself and effective in compelling the necessary degree of cooperation among nations in matters of resources, trade, monetary arrangements, population, food, the oceans, and the atmosphere—not to mention attaining justice for peoples and insuring orderly change. Rather, it appears that power will be diffused to the point that it will become unmanageable in itself and unusable in influencing—or coercing, if necessary—constructive behavior in economic, social, environmental, and political areas.

2. The international system will probably continue to degenerate into a disorder more severe than we have known. Almost certainly it will not stabilize in some neat, balanced configuration of three or four or five nations or groups, coordinating on basic objectives and competing according to rules that are benign for the system as a whole—in short, a balance of power. Instead, this process is likely to proceed to a kaleidoscopic interaction of multiple political entities.

By all measures of power—military (nuclear or conventional, actual or potential), economic (total wealth or commercial weight), or political (the will to autonomy and achievement)—there may be fifteen or twenty salient states, not necessarily equal and not necessarily armed with nuclear weapons, but potent to the point of enjoying the possibility of independent action.

3. Few if any governing groups will have enough legitimacy to induce their nations to support actions for the sake of international order that are not in the obvious and immediate interest of the nation itself. As a particular case, the American public is unlikely to understand and support, or remain acquiescent in, even the lower scale of sacrifices and the more subtle risks involved in a balance of power policy. And we are unlikely to coordinate the elements of our own political system or to forge a sufficient consensus to respond to marginal challenges that structurally approximate Vietnam.

4. Much the same conditions pertain in economic and social areas. Efforts by the United States and other well-endowed and competent (or simply privileged) nations to mitigate the misfortunes, inadequacies, or even follies of the rest of the world would be diluted long before they could have decisive effect. Conversely, though we ought to give a large amount of help, a sufficient amount, translated into sacrifices by the populations of donor nations, would be socially and politically unacceptable in those nations.

5. Thus, the United States and other analogously situated nations will probably look increasingly to their own security and welfare, counting on their own resources and, where these fail, relying on their own initiatives in strategic and economic diplomacy.

6. These tendencies will lead to a somewhat worse state of affairs—a second-best order of things—for all.

This is a kind of international system, very different from the one we have become accustomed to since 1945. We have to get used to a world that cannot be controlled by us, a world where we don't have the ability, let alone the right, to act out our needs for national self-esteem. It will be a world of parameters (intractable, recalcitrant circumstances), not preferences; a world shaped by constraints, not commitments.

On this score, the "new Wilsonians," the American moral-expansionists, are missing the point.[2] I have no quarrel with the values of the Wilsonians. What I do have is a disagreement about the function of foreign policy. Beyond this, I sense that the Wilsonians are caught in a methodological trap. They posit a preferred outcome or an acceptable range of decent outcomes. They then embrace policies that seem to lead to this preferred state of affairs and implicitly veto any suggested course that leads to something else. (They differ from the "realists," who also do these things, in that they suffuse their preferred outcome with moral significance.) The argument of the noninterventionists—my argument—stresses the constraints of our domestic situation and the parameters of the international system. It acknowledges (1) that these constraints and parameters are increasingly rigid and unfavorable, in themselves, to the possibility of active, influential foreign policies, and (2) that they reinforce each other. For example, the worsening cost-benefit ratio of influencing an international situation by intervention in turn makes domestic support for intervention even more difficult to obtain.

For a second-best world, there are several general policy prescriptions.

1. In the world economy, we should preserve autonomy of national decision making and achieve relative freedom from vulnerabilities. This does not equate to a policy of instant autarky, but it does suggest an approach, within our means —much more than we have done so far—toward the capacity for self-sufficiency. We should place greater weight on developing specific hedges against the pressures and deprivations that may be occasioned by the hostility or opportunism or simple incompetence of other nations. (In other words,

we might protect our security far better by eliminating vulnerabilities than by creating interdependencies.) This is also far from precluding cooperative efforts to attain workable and livable regimes in the many functional areas where such cooperation is preferable to purely national solutions. But this prescription does warn against expecting so much from present efforts at international cooperation that we fail to anticipate and discount critical noncompliance by other nations.

2. In international politics, we should achieve the flexibility to avoid conflict by divesting rather than acquiring commitments in situations we cannot control, and by providing insulation from the outcomes of situations we cannot afford to control.

This process of disengagement would not end until we had found a new, obviously defensible security frontier. We would have to reconcile ourselves to diminished weight in the international system—to let allies make their own accommodations, to do some hedging of our own against their defections, and perhaps even to let our adversaries have their season of mischief in the world.

This is not tantamount to leaving the United States defenseless. It is simply to recognize that an alternative way to avoid the domino effect is to put some space between the dominoes, to get the first ones to stand up by themselves, and to make the final domino—ourselves—invulnerable to a host of pressures, and correspondingly resistant to the temptation to intervene.

Nor is this a matter of waffling on the "threat." Such a policy of disengagement does not proceed from any hopeful estimates of a new era, where threats have disappeared or have become muted through the internal reform of our adversaries or their adherence to external rules of the game— the twin illusions of detente. Nor does it imply that intervention will become unnecessary because we will develop other mechanisms or institutions for solving international problems, such as a more perfect and potent United Nations or an efficient condominium of superpowers. Quite the contrary. We will continue to experience what can be taken as strategic challenges. There will still be potential vulnerabilities for ourselves and consequently temptations for others. And there will be no sure rescue in collective security (international organization) or collective defense (alliances). Indeed, the saving argument that nothing will happen anyway is not an adequate condition for any policy, whether one of disengagement or intervention.

Rather, a policy of disengagement would accept a divisible peace, some reverses to our positions, and a loss of our special control over the course of the entire system. The real point is that, if we are willing to take a long future-perfect view (looking back from some point perhaps twenty to forty years from now), we may realize that, whether we intervene or disengage, oppose or acquiesce, we can live with or cope with a wide range of plausible outcomes. Conversely, from that intellectual vantage point in the future, the difference between the best and the worst of the plausible outcomes may seem less than the cost of causing the best to happen—even the cost of successful deterrence (except, of course, the deterrence of central nuclear war).

Predicting future systems and alternative worlds puts into perspective some assumptions about the scope and permanence—and the inevitability—of American interests. The presumption that still goes unchallenged is that America's actual and proper concerns are universal. This presumption has become a special part of the myth of America's uniqueness as a nation and a force in the world. Indeed, the corollary that there can be no solutions that are not American solutions perhaps reached its apogee in Kissinger's ubiquitous shuttle diplomacy and worldwide orchestration, and continues in the "architectural" ambitions of the Carter administration. But interests are not absolute. They are somewhat circular: America's assertion of interests has justified its exercise of power, and, in turn, the exercise of power has validated the assertion of interests.

At the moment, I suppose one could argue that our power still runs with our pretensions to create and support extensive order in the world. Indeed, the agricultural and technological deficiencies of our adversaries and the uneven incidence of oil dependencies and monetary burdens on our allies may have given the United States a relative advantage and a new lease on its economic and political ascendancy. But it is increasingly likely that American power will fall short of this universal scope, whether through external opposition, excessive cost, or insufficient domestic support.

The question, then, is not directly whether we choose to continue to command global interests but, more indirectly and more fundamentally, whether we will continue to have the means and the competence, and whether our government's diverse constituency will continue to grant it a clear delegation of authority, to pursue such interests.

The answers to those questions will determine America's role in the international system and will define its new range of interests in the world.

Notes

Chapter 1. Collective Amnesia or Perpetual Debate?

1. *New York Times*, Op-Ed, June 29, 1975.

2. The point is further documented by Henry Kissinger's plea to the Subcommittee on African Affairs of the Senate Committee on Foreign Relations, January 29, 1976, for approval of covert assistance to a faction in Angola: "We are told that by providing money and arms to Angola we are duplicating the mistakes we made in Viet-Nam. Such an argument confuses the expenditure of tens of millions of dollars with the commitment of U. S. troops. If we accept such a gross distortion of history—if we accept the claim that we can no longer do anything to aid our friends abroad because we will inevitably do too much—then the tragedy of Viet-Nam will indeed be monumental." (*Department of State Bulletin*, February 16, 1976, p. 181.)

3. Each type of lesson is elaborated in a separate chapter in Part 2 of this book. Of course, these types of lessons are really constructs—syndromes of attitudes held by various groupings. They are not mutually exclusive in all respects. For example, the same individual critic can harbor "fundamental" objections to the tendencies of American diplomacy along with elements of a "consequential" critique (that savings from the defense budget translate into commitments to domestic welfare). Or a critic could subscribe to the "proportional" thesis (that the nation's interests were not worth so much sacrifice) in combination with an "instrumental" analysis, and arrive at the conclusion that, if a war would be won with a few divisions in a couple of months (as Robert Kennedy once impatiently suggested in the early 1960s), then such an excursion might be justified. But the classifi-

cation presented here is "operational": it represents the various critiques of Vietnam, intervention, and the American military posture and foreign policy in ways that imply differences in the remedies.

4. The five alternative critiques are succinctly represented in Table 1.

5. Most explanations of the past and most prescriptions for the future suffer from conceptual disorders: misconceptions of the nature of policy and misapprehensions of the structure and process of policy choice. For this reason, this book inevitably has a theoretical, as well as a practical, cast. In fact, it suggests a theory of foreign policy choice and the determination of national action.

6. Such a model, illustrating America's adjustment to the constraints revealed by Vietnam, and a discussion of the process represented by this model, are presented in Chapter 5.

7. Such a "new consensus" was announced by the Public Agenda Foundation and hailed by the editors of the *New York Times* (September 18, 1976). This consensus contains such contradictions as: "vigorous pursuit of detente, but without making any inequitable concessions to the Soviets," "establishment of diplomatic relations with The People's Republic of China, but without abandoning Taiwan," "U. S. support for defending human rights more vigorously and . . . for advocating our own democratic values against competing ideological systems" but "without being preacher or policeman." The report cited a "widespread agreement on principles," but could explain the "unusual disarray in our foreign policy" only by references to "complexity," "lack of knowledge," and "genuine disagreement on how certain principles should be implemented"—which means, of course, that there is no real operational agreement on the principles themselves. Indeed, one of the participating experts concluded that "the most basic foreign policy task of any future administration must be the 'successful management of contradictions' in a manner that elicits public support"—a prescription that, besides being breathtakingly optimistic, is in itself a contradiction.

8. Though the radical fundamentalists overstate the requirement for social and institutional change and ignore the strategic conditions for the moral shift on which they insist. (See my critique in Chapters 4 and 8.)

Chapter 2. Lessons about Lessons: Cat on a Hot Coal Stove

1. "What the War Was About," the *Observer* (London), January 28, 1973.

2. Quoted in Arthur M. Schlesinger, Jr., *The Bitter Heritage: Vietnam and American Democracy*, 1941–1966 (Greenwich, Connecticut: Fawcett, 1968), p. 99.

3. "Foreign Policy For Disillusioned Liberals," *Foreign Policy* (Winter 1972–73). Note also Walter Laqueur ("The World and President Carter," *Commentary*, February 1978), who complains: "The dead hand of Vietnam still weighs heavily on the American memory, and the fear of involvement in some dubious foreign adventure still clouds much of the thinking of official Washington. It is the old story of the cat which, once burned, never approached a stove again."

4. *A World Restored: The Politics of Conservatism in a Revolutionary Age* (New York: The Universal Library, 1964), p. 331.

5. "Military Intervention, Political Involvement, and the Unlessons of Vietnam," Chicago: Adlai Stevenson Institute of International Affairs, Monograph, 1968, pp. 1, 2.

6. "The Domestic Scene," in Robert E. Osgood et al., *America and the World: From the Truman Doctrine to Vietnam* (Baltimore: Johns Hopkins University Press, 1970), p. 187.

7. "Learning the Wrong Lessons," February 1, 1975.

8. In Zagoria's article, "Why We Can't Leave Korea," *New York Times Magazine*, October 2, 1977. A point similar to all the above is made more broadly by Ernest R. May, *"Lessons" of the Past: The Use and Misuse of History in American Foreign Policy* (New York: Oxford, 1973).

9. To pose these questions in a philosophical way is to invoke the ancient problem—the most fundamental epistemological as well as metaphysical problem—of the One and the Many. We experience diversity, but we also see things as continuities, wholes, indentities, and we see them as belonging to categories. Of course, no two observed things, or instances, are quite the same. The question is this: Is the diversity real and therefore not subject to composition or even definition (not to mention the problem of explaining how the diverse things were generated in the first place)? Or is the diversity merely illusory—a contention that solves the metaphysical problem of the generation of diverse things (by denying it) but creates the epistemological problem of how, and why, we differentiate anything from everything else?

The extreme exponent of the latter position was Parmenides, who held that reality was one and unchanging and who, correspondingly, had trouble explaining the impression—and the evolution—of diversity. The extreme exponent of the former position was Heraclitus, who said that everything is in flux; even apparent identity (such as river from moment to moment) is a fiction; one cannot step into the same river again—it is not the same, at two different moments, in two different observations. Therefore he had trouble explaining how we do, in fact, discern dimensions, or common principles, in series of changing and unlike things.

10. "The Lessons of Vietnam: Have We Learned, or Only Failed?" *New York Times Magazine*, April 1, 1973. See the extended discussion of the proportional critique in Chapter 6.

11. Among the benefits to the South Koreans: waiver of "MAP transfer" (the shifting of military operation and maintenance costs to the Koreans), equalization payments, direct budgetary subsidies, favored treatment among military grant aid recipients, and retention of American forces in Korea at full strength during most of the Vietnam war.

12. *Mandate for Change* (New York: Signet, 1963), p. 450.

Chapter 3. Overworking the Munich Analogy

1. July 28, 1965. Cited in F. M. Kail, *What Washington Said: Administration Rhetoric and the Vietnam War* (New York: Harper and Row, 1973), p. 80.

2. "A Miserable Choice," *Washington Post*, October 12, 1972.

3. "McGovern's Peace Terms," *New York Times*, October 11, 1972.

4. In a review article of Joseph Buttinger, *Vietnam: The Unforgettable Tragedy* (New York: Horizon Press, 1977), in *New Republic*, June 11, 1977.

5. "Churchill and Us," *Commentary*, June, 1977.

6. For an interesting account of the failure of deterrence in September 1939, see Alan Alexandroff and Richard Rosecrance, "Deterrence in 1939," *World Politics*, April 1977.

7. This construction of Munich derives much from the interpretation of A. J. P. Taylor, *The Origins of the Second World War*, 2d ed. (Greenwich, Connecticut: Fawcett, 1961), particularly pp. 156 ff. This interpretation is corroborated from the German side in General Halder's recollections at the Nuremberg Trial: "Now came Mr. Chamberlain and with one stroke the danger of war was ended. . . ." (Quoted in Allen W. Dulles, *The German Underground*, New York, 1947, p. 47.)

Chapter 4. Was Vietnam a Mistake?

1. Ball, Memorandum to Rusk, McNamara, and McGeorge Bundy (TOP SECRET), reprinted as "Top Secret: The Prophecy the President Rejected," in *The Atlantic*, July 1972.

2. An example is Robert L. Gallucci, *Neither Peace nor Honor: The Politics of American Military Policy in Vietnam* (Baltimore: Johns Hopkins, 1975).

3. This kind of analysis and prescription also appears in Alexander L. George, "The Case for Multiple Advocacy in Making Foreign Policy," *American Political Science Review*, September 1972, pp. 751–785. George's analysis, however, also recognizes ideological and cognitive factors, and his far-reaching prescription for restructuring presidential advice and decision making itself has cognitive aspects and might be seen almost as a kind of "strategic" remedy.

4. "Vietnam: The System Worked," *Foreign Policy*, Summer 1971.

5. Ball, Memorandum to Rusk et al.

6. *Papers on the War* (New York: Simon and Schuster, 1972), especially the introduction and the chapter, "The Quagmire Myth and the Stalemate Machine," taken from Ellsberg's article by the same title in *Public Policy*, Spring 1971, and in turn from his paper, "Escalating in a Quagmire," presented at the American Political Science Association, Los Angeles, September 1970.

7. *The Bitter Heritage: Vietnam and American Democracy, 1941–1966.*

8. Though Ellsberg himself has come to see that Schlesinger's model and his own are not quite as antithetical and mutually exclusive as he first sensed they were. See Ellsberg's comments (*Papers on the War*, p. 27) on the plausibility of some of Schlesinger's arguments in the latter's "Eyeless in Indochina," *New York Review of Books*, October 21, 1971.

9. By syllogistic logic, the affirmation of the necessary condition in its pure form ("no immorality") is sufficient to bring about the effect ("therefore, no intervention").

10. This logical statement (and the one below, relating America's eco-

nomic-institutional structure to intervention as a sufficient condition) might suggest that both the independent and dependent variables are dichotomous (either-or). Actually, the variables can be continuous. But even if they are taken as continuous, there is a point at which the response (nonintervention or intervention) "flops over." In any case, it should be understood that these stark logical statements are illustrative and represent probable responses and effects, not certainties.

11. We can derive a necessary condition from a sufficient condition by double negation: if there is *not* the condition of *no* capitalist institutions, then there will *not* be the effect of *no* intervention. In other words (the more normal statement of a necessary condition), *only if* there are no capitalist institutions will there be no interventions.

12. It is possible that Marxists are asserting institutional factors as both sufficient and necessary conditions for repressive interventions. I doubt this, but Ole R. Holsti, in a critical article, "The Study of International Politics Makes Strange Bedfellows: Theories of the Radical Right and the Radical Left," *American Political Science Review*, March 1974, p. 233, seems to believe it: "On the left there is a consistent call for revolutionary transformation of capitalist America as a *necessary and sufficient* condition for solving mankind's most pressing moral and social problems" (italics added). This judgment, and others in Holsti's article, refer to radical explanations of American intervention.

13. Though subsequently he has been drawn to the thesis of economic-institutional causation (from a discussion with Ellsberg, July 1977).

14. *Papers on the War*, pp. 305 ff.

15. *Papers on the War*, p. 38.

16. Perhaps I should clarify my attitude toward moral constraints. I favor the rigorous strengthening of moral constraints on foreign policy. I simply doubt that they alone will be sufficient (especially in extreme cases of strategic challenge) to preclude national responses that lead to intervention and that consequently create situations that render immoral conduct more probable, both on our own part and throughout the international system. Since, in my view, intervention is dominated by *strategic* premises and motives, a noninterventionist policy must appropriately be built on revised strategic presumptions.

I treat moral constraints as independent and additional to more restrictive strategic presumptions—as a kind of "double lock" on national conduct. I want moral constraints to operate (1) in the same direction as the strategic presumptions—that is, toward a noninterventionist national policy—and (2) in a consistent philosophical framework that will be conducive to a universal regime of nonintervention.

Chapter 5. The Establishment's Response: Better Instruments

1. The concept of depletion is from Seymour Melman, *Our Depleted Society* (New York: Holt, Rinehart and Winston, 1965), and *Pentagon Capitalism: The Political Economy of War* (New York: McGraw-Hill, 1970).

2. This lesson is a novel one in post-Second World War American politics. As Bruce M. Russett pointed out in *What Price Vigilance? The Burdens of*

National Defense (New Haven: Yale, 1970, pp. 23–24), both on the eve of previous conflicts and after extended periods of peace the American public has preponderantly rejected the notion that defense budgets were too high (in 1960 only 18% thought they were) and has favored increased defense outlays (in 1950 more than 60% did). Only by 1969 did a majority (52%) wish to reduce the existing level of defense expenditures (American Institute of Public Opinion press release, August 14, 1969).

3. The peak total defense budget (in actual outlays) during the Vietnam war, in 1968, was about $79 billion, or 8.7% of the gross national product (cf. 9.4% in the Secretary of Defense Report). The peak budget of the Korean war in 1953 was $48 billion, or 13% of GNP. The peak of the Second World War in 1944 was $87 billion, or 35% of GNP (1942 and 1943, though absolutely lower, were 42%). (Figures are from Russett, *What Price Vigilance?*)

4. See John R. Probert, "The Reserves and National Guard: Their Changing Role in National Defense," in John P. Lovell and Philip S. Kronenberg, eds., *New Civil-Military Relations* (New Brunswick, N. J.: Transaction Books, 1974). The Nixon-Laird regime reverted to the policy of mobilizing reserve units, rather than the draft, as the primary emerging method of augmenting forces. But this policy has not been tested by events.

5. This is not to say that defense outlays of $78, $86, $89, $96, $105, and $115 billion for fiscal years 1974, 1975, 1976, 1977, 1978, and 1979 are small, in absolute economic terms, or that 19 land divisions and 44 tactical air wings including 12 carrier groups are a pitiful or second-best force. But they are smaller than the force of the 1960s and have less weight as a percentage of a rising gross national product (outlays declined to about 5.1% of GNP for fiscal year 1979, compared with 9.4% for FY 1968, and 8.3% for FY 1964—but only 4.5% for FY 1950). (Figures are from Secretary of Defense, Annual Defense Reports.)

6. The "top priority" Army weapons system and development programs for the 1970s included: helicopter gunships (mostly in an antitank role), helicopter lift for tactical mobility, antitank weapons, a new sophisticated main battle tank, an improved surface-to-air missile, electronic "automated battlefield" capabilities for information generation and control, more accurate and lethal conventional artillery munitions, and technically improved target acquisition systems for maneuver units and artillery commanders (*Armed Forces Journal*, November 16, 1970, pp. 19–23).

7. A good summary of these technological lessons appeared in George C. Wilson, "Hard-Learned Lessons In a Military Laboratory," *Washington Post* special section on Vietnam, January 28, 1973.

8. See the Hearings of the Electronic Battlefield Subcommittee of the Preparedness Investigating Subcommittee of the Committee on Armed Services, U. S. Senate, February 22, 1971. For a lively journalistic account, see Paul Dickson and John Rothchild, "The Electronic Battlefield: Wiring Down the War," *Washington Monthly*, May 1971. See also Paul Dickson's book, *The Electronic Battlefield* (Bloomington: Indiana University Press, 1976).

9. Sulzberger, "Solving an Ugly Dilemma," *New York Times*, Section 4, November 15, 1970; and "The New Nuclear Look II," *New York Times*, Jan-

Notes

uary 10, 1971. Robert M. Lawrence, "On Tactical Nuclear War," *Revue Militaire Generale*, January and February 1971.

10. Quoted in Walter Pincus, "Why More Nukes?" *New Republic*, February 9, 1974.

11. Hearings of the Senate Foreign Relations Subcommittee on U. S. Security Agreements and Commitments Abroad, reported as "Enthoven, Warnke Attack Tactical A-Arms in Europe," *Washington Post*, March 15, 1974. On the other hand, the U. S. representative to the 26-nation disarmament talks at Geneva assured the participants "categorically" that the United States had "no intention whatever" of developing mini-nukes that would be "interchangeable with conventional arms." And Congress refused the Pentagon $1 billion of funds requested for FY 1975 for producing more accurate and less explosive nuclear munitions for 8-inch and 155-mm. artillery. (Michael Getler, "U. S. Offers 'Mini-Nuke' Assurance," *Washington Post*, May 24, 1974.) It is not to be thought, however, that "clean" low-yield weapons imply the absence of radiation. Quite the contrary (as pointed out in a meticulous calculation of casualty criteria and disability syndromes, by Captain Arnold S. Warshawsky, "Radiation Battlefield Casualties—Credible!!" *Military Review*, May 1976): "With modern low-yield tactical nuclear weapons, nuclear radiation has replaced air blast as the dominant casualty-producing effect, thereby reducing the degree of collateral damage. . . . Thus, the characteristics of modern low-yield tactical weapons increase the credibility of the US strategy of flexible nuclear response to Warsaw Pact aggressions." This early discussion, in the technical military literature, foreshadowed the emergence of the "neutron bomb" (actually a high-radiation artillery shell or short-range missile warhead) in the early Carter administration.

12. "Defense Debate Focuses on Kind of War to Plan For," *New York Times*, March 18, 1974.

13. Capt. Raymond S. Blunt and Capt. Thomas O. Cason, "Realistic Doctrine: Basic Thinking Today," *Air University Review*, May–June 1973, reporting on *Air Force Manual 1-1: United States Air Force Basic Doctrine*, September 28, 1971.

14. Lt. Col. Joseph F. Santilli, Jr., U. S. Army, "NATO Strategy Updated: A First Use Policy," *Military Review*, March 1974.

15. "Mini-Nukes and Strategy," *International Journal*, spring 1974.

16. "A Credible Nuclear-Emphasis Defense for NATO," *Orbis*, summer 1973.

17. "Nuclear Weapons and 'Flexible Response'," *Orbis*, summer 1970.

18. "The Realities of Tactical Nuclear Warfare," *Orbis*, summer 1973.

19. *Strategic Power and National Security* (Pittsburgh, Pa.: University of Pittsburgh Press, 1971), p. 117.

20. For a concise assessment of various tactical nuclear postures in Europe, see Jeffrey Record, *U. S. Nuclear Weapons in Europe: Issues and Alternatives* (Washington, D. C.: Brookings, 1975).

21. In connection with this change of attitude within the Army, there has been a decline in the organizational status of those branches (such as the Green Berets) which enjoyed a brief prominence during the early stages of

the Vietnam war. To survive, such branches have tried to mechanize—that is, to become airmobile, high-firepower units—as in the 1970 Sontay operation in collaboration with their Air Force counterparts, the Special Operations Force. A new organization of U. S. Army Rangers, called Black Berets, now trains to execute "Entebbe-type" long-range strike operations. The former counter-insurgency branches have also adopted new functions, such as military assistance, paramedic, and public works.

22. In the case of Sontay, the *Washington Post* reported that neither the National Security Council nor the Washington Special Action Group were collectively consulted, nor were ranking State Department officials in charge of the prisoner issue even informed. (November 29, 1970)

23. On the subject of cooptation of, rather than consultation with, Congress, note the advice to the president by Assistant Secretary of State William P. Bundy on November 5, 1964: "Congress must be consulted before any major action perhaps only by notification . . . but preferably by talks with . . . key leaders. . . . We probably do not need additional congressional authority even if we decide on very strong action." (Quoted by Congressman Les Aspin, *Washington Post* editorial page, October 31, 1973.)

24. An example was the Pentagon plan for the wholesale closure or consolidation of bases in Japan, including some of the largest facilities there, such as the airbases at Tachikawa, Misawa, and Yokota, and the naval air station at Atsugi. The essentials of this plan had been recommended within the Office of the Secretary of Defense in late 1968 and bitterly contested by the services, the Joint Chiefs of Staff, and the theater commands. In comparatively leaner times, under Secretary Laird, the plan was accepted by the military.

25. These symptoms have been called *Uptonianism* (after General Emory Upton, U. S. Army, who wrote around the last quarter of the nineteenth century). A debate about the prospects for Uptonianism has been conducted in the pages of the Army's journal, *Military Review*. See particularly the summary article, "Future Civil-Military Relations: The Army Turns Inward?" by Lt. Col. John H. Moellering, U. S. Army, in the July 1973 issue.

26. See Ben A. Franklin, "Lag in a Volunteer Force Spurs Talk of New Draft," *New York Times*, July 1, 1973.

27. But a RAND study in late 1977 concluded that "the number of blacks entering the armed forces would be about the same under the all-volunteer force or the draft." *New York Times*, September 26, 1977.)

28. But see also Andrew Uscher, "Cost of the All Volunteer Force," *Armed Forces Journal*, April 1974. His analysis demonstrates that 95% of increased military pay costs over the past ten years are attributable rather to the "comparability process" (with pay scales in private industry), not to the ending of the draft, and would continue even if the draft were reinstated; that the "opportunity cost" of the all-volunteer force is only $306 million a year; and that, because of additional training costs, a return to the draft would actually save only about $50 million a year.

29. See Martin Binkin's analysis in Joseph A. Pechman, ed., *The 1978 Budget: Setting National Priorities* (Washington, D.C.: Brookings, 1977), pp. 126–134.

30. *New York Times* editorial, January 26, 1977.

31. Charles De Gaulle (when a lieutenant colonel), in his 1934 work, *Toward a Professional Army*, had advocated a small professional armored force designed to meet the most probable intermediate-scale contingencies of the interwar period. After the Second World War, France achieved its small, professional force, though it was optimized for colonial (Indochina and Algeria) rather than European interventions. This force subsequently overthrew the Fourth Republic in 1958 and very nearly overthrew the Fifth Republic several years later. Only the admixture of potentially undisciplined, socially-oriented conscripts in the French army in 1960 saved De Gaulle's own regime.

32. Capt. Wayne P. Hughes, Jr., "Vietnam: Winnable War?" in *Proceedings of the U. S. Naval Institute*, July 1977.

33. Tabulated in July 1977 by Professors Rosenau, Holsti, and Verba of Duke, Southern California, and Harvard Universities.

34. *U. S. News & World Report*, May 26, 1975, p. 25.

35. The term has been used by Col. Richard F. Rosser, "American Civil-Military Relations in the 1980s," in Richard G. Head and Ervin J. Rokke, eds., *American Defense Policy* (Baltimore: Johns Hopkins, 1973).

36. Public survey conducted by the Institute for Social Research at the University of Michigan, cited in the *Washington Post*, May 9, 1974.

37. A cooler attitude of the young potential elites toward the exercise of American power—particularly toward the use of military force to salvage certain nations or strategic positions—was described by Graham T. Allison in "Cool It: The Foreign Policy of Young America," *Foreign Policy*, winter 1970-1971. But the significance of this cooler attitude is still open to question. In Allison's own interpretation, this attitude portends a more restricted, inhibited American role in the world. But does this imply a benign, and negligent, withdrawal from positions of strength and an unconditional disregard for potential foreign threats? Or does it imply the substitution of aseptic force signified by the Nixon Doctrine, the more subtle manipulation of power marked by Kissinger's diplomacy, and the devolution of personal military service to the less privileged classes embodied in the concept of the volunteer army? A more recent straw in the wind is an opinion poll taken among the Freshman class at Yale in 1976, which "found that 40 per cent of Yale's freshmen felt the student protest movements of the 1960s had hurt the country" (reported in the *Washington Post*, October 16, 1977).

38. The restoration of bipartisan foreign policy management in the Congress, as sought by Secretary of State Kissinger in his address to the Los Angeles World Affairs Council on January 24, 1975 (*Department of State Bulletin*, February 17, 1975, pp. 197-204), would amount to the replacement of the creative, though often obstructive, congressional regime by a privileged consultative oligarchy that might sanctify interventionist initiatives by the Executive Branch.

39. For an early report on the increasing role of the military in forming national strategy, see Neil Sheehan, "Influence of Joint Chiefs Is Reported Rising," *New York Times*, June 30, 1969. Lawrence J. Korb ("The Secretary of Defense and the Joint Chiefs of Staff in the Nixon Administration: The Method and the Men," in John P. Lovell and Philip S. Kronenberg, eds.,

New Civil-Military Relations, New Brunswick, N.J.: Transaction, 1974) documents the deference of the Nixon-Laird administration to the strategic and budgetary predilections of the JCS. One notable departure under Nixon and Laird was that the chiefs were able to appeal—often successfully—the completed Defense Department budget to the Defense Program Review Committee (DPRC) of the National Security Council. Under McNamara, final defense budgets could not be altered by higher review. And under still prior administrations, the defense budget was often cut but never raised at the initiative of the military. Nevertheless, Korb's own conclusion is that the changes in procedure under Nixon and Laird were minor and were only throwbacks to the pre-McNamara era. Also notable, in the Nixon and subsequent administrations, has been the increased presence in policy-making positions in the (nominally civilian) Office of the Secretary of Defense of generals and admirals on active duty.

40. An early expression of this change was the replacement of the Draft Presidential Memorandums (DPMs), initiated in the Office of Systems Analysis, by a new programming document, the Joint Force Memorandum (JFM), prepared by the Joint Chiefs of Staff with specifiic inputs from the services after they have received fiscal guidance by the Secretary of Defense. (Of course, the fiscal guidance itself was still based on staff work by Systems Analysis.) In the second Nixon administration, Systems Analysis briefly lost, then recovered, its status as a separate assistant-secretaryship, and its name was changed to Program Analysis and Evaluation.

41. Gilbert W. Fitzhugh et al. (the "Blue Ribbon Defense Panel"), *Report to the President and the Secretary of Defense on the Department of Defense ("Defense for Peace")*, Washington, D.C.: U. S. Government Printing Office, July 1970.

42. Though another far-reaching study of the possible overhaul of the Joint Chiefs of Staff is being conducted by the civilian defense officials of the Carter administration (*New York Times*, November 8, 1977); and President Carter has requested the Chiefs to give their advice to him through the Secretary of Defense. It remains to be seen whether, to what extent, and how permanently these initiatives will change the substantive weight of military preferences for force structures, weapons systems, and strategic doctrines in the formulation of defense and foreign policy.

Chapter 6. The Liberal Critique: A Sense of Proportion

1. See the memorandum of Assistant Secretary of State William P. Bundy, November 1964, cited in Daniel Ellsberg, *Papers on the War* (New York: Simon and Schuster, 1972), p. 33.

2. "The Lessons of Vietnam: Have We Learned, or Only Failed?" *New York Times Magazine*, April 1, 1973.

3. Chapter 2.

4. Memorandum to Rusk, McNamara, and McGeorge Bundy (TOP SECRET), reprinted as "Top Secret: The Prophecy the President Rejected," in the *Atlantic*, July 1972. There is no evidence that Ball attempted to put this memorandum before President Johnson until January 1965.

5. "Legacy of the Cold War in Indochina," *Foreign Affairs*, July 1970.

Hoopes' adherence to the proportionalist thesis is illustrated by his judgments:

". . . at each of several critical junctures [1962, 1963, 1964] . . . American leadership failed to grasp the central truth: namely, that the U. S. interest in Southeast Asia is limited, not vital; that while a limited effort to shore up South Vietnam was warranted, a total effort to save a government founded at low tide upon the receding sands of the French colonial empire was both alien to our interest and destructive of our reputation.

"North Vietnam's unexpected tenacity, deriving from the fact that the war was for Hanoi a vital struggle, led us in the event to the application of progressively unlimited means. This loss of proportion led to wanton destruction, to a gross disparity between ends and means, and therein lies the immorality."

6. The apparent problem can be resolved by distinguishing among the dimensions of *limits*: (a) duration, (b) geographical extension, (c) linear extension or intensity, a quantitative increase in the application of resources, (d) technological escalation (such as to tactical nuclear weapons) or a qualitative leap to a different plane of warfare.

Chapter 7. The Economic Argument: Consequences and "Priorities"

1. It also turns out that a large number of American corporate executives subscribe to a consequential critique of Vietnam. As Bruce M. Russett and Betty C. Hanson reported in their survey of 600 vice presidents of America's largest companies ("How Corporate Executives See America's Role in the World," *Fortune*, May 1974): 53 percent stated that they thought it incorrect for the United States to send ground combat troops to Vietnam, while only 37 percent agreed with this decision. "86 percent thought the war was 'bad' for 'American social and political institutions.' And 77 percent thought it was bad for the economy . . . The executives are not anxious to undertake another war that might have similar consequences."

2. Of course, there have been many analyses and commentaries that serve mostly to demonstrate the costs and consequences of the military exercises and preparations of the past quarter-century, or the kinds of trade-offs involved in developing or purchasing certain individual weapons systems. Good examples of such studies are Marion Anderson, "The Empty Pork Barrel: Unemployment and the Pentagon Budget," Lansing, Michigan: Public Interest Research Group In Michigan (PIRGIM), April 1975; Seymour Melman, several books referred to above, and "Twelve Propositions on Productivity and War Economy," *Armed Forces and Society*, August 1975; and Robert Warren Stevens, *Vain Hopes, Grim Realities: The Economic Consequences of the Vietnam War* (New York: New Viewpoints, 1976). Such demonstrations do not in themselves constitute "the consequential critique" unless they also assert or imply (1) that what has been principally wrong with our interventionist posture is these costs, consequences, trade-offs, and distorted priorities; (2) that restoring "correct" priorities will also improve our foreign and military policies; and (3) that reducing the burdens of defense will, virtually automatically, release resources that will be applied to

other areas of the economy. It is upon the logic of these propositions that I focus this discussion.

3. *American Political Science Review*, June 1969, pp. 412–426; also presented in his book, *What Price Vigilance? The Burdens of National Defense* (New Haven: Yale, 1970), chaps. 5 and 6, pp. 127–177. Russett relates defense spending to gross national product rather than to the distribution of income and taxes. Thus the question he addresses is really *"what* pays for defense?"

It would be unfair to Russett to say that he *strictly* conditions more ample domestic programs on the reduction of defense spending. He actually uses his research conclusions to *plead for* "insensitivity" of government health and education expenditures to the size of the defense budget, citing the positive experience of other governments (such as those of Britain and France) in keeping these expenditures autonomous. Russett hedges again—and properly—in this respect, in saying (*APSR*, p. 422): "The relationships we have discovered in past American experience suggest what the costs of future military efforts may be. These relationships are of course not immutable." Russett also inserts the hedge (p. 433), in explaining that the Canadian case differs diametrically from the American in exhibiting a *positive* correlation between defense spending and private investment: "It is impossible to tell from this kind of analysis whether the tradeoff is the result of deliberate and explicit policy." But this is one of the essential points of my criticism: a neglect of deliberate policy choice is the crucial flaw in the consequential model. I return to this point below.

I certainly have no quarrel with Russett's data and procedures, his scheme of hypotheses, and the quality of his variables. My purpose is to present a logical, not technical, argument and a general airing of the important implications of the consequentialist model.

4. I do not mean to ignore or diminish the case that a grave casualty of a militarized economy is fixed private capital formation. This phenomenon is the "depletion" described by Seymour Melman in *Our Depleted Society* (New York: Holt, Rinehart and Winston, 1965) and *Pentagon Capitalism: The Political Economy of War* (New York: McGraw-Hill, 1970).

5. In any case, expenditures on welfare relate (as we would expect) inversely to defense expenditures, though for a somewhat different reason—defense booms relieve unemployment and so reduce the demand for welfare payments, not the supply.

6. Of course, generically, or in a pure mathematical definition, both manifestations of constraints are trade-offs or parameters (expressions of what one item is worth in relation to another item or by some absolute measure).

7. The actual acceptance of this alternative by the Johnson administration from 1965 on, rather than either of the two other basic alternatives, has been severely criticized by the economist Robert Warren Stevens, *Vain Hopes, Grim Realities*. In the consequentialist argument, the way the Vietnam war was financed becomes as serious a matter as the war itself.

8. As Russett points out: "Education usually suffers very immediately when the military needs to expand sharply; it recovers its share only slowly after defense spending has peaked. . . . [Health expenditures] lost out to

the exigencies of defense in the early 1950's and bounced back slowly, at the same rate as did education." (*APSR*, pp. 420–421) Actually the claim has been made by Barry Blechman and others that the decline in defense expenditures, "as measured in constant dollars . . . by one-third from the Vietnam War peak [to fiscal year 1977] . . . proved to be an important source for financing both domestic programs and tax reductions." (Barry M. Blechman et al., "The Defense Budget," in Joseph A. Pechman, ed., *The 1978 Budget: Setting National Priorities*, Washington, D.C.: Brookings, 1977, p. 82.)

9. This squares with Russett's observation that after every war the new basic level of defense spending, as a percentage of GNP, has been double the prewar level (*APSR*, p. 414).

Chapter 8. The Fundamentalists: Morality and Institutional Change

1. Joyce and Gabriel Kolko, *The Limits of Power: The World and United States Foreign Policy, 1945–1954* (New York: Harper and Row, 1972), p. 8.

2. The phrase is from Richard J. Barnet, *Intervention and Revolution* (New York: World, 1968), p. 283. In his *Roots of War* (New York: Atheneum, 1972), Barnet presents an articulate, somewhat eclectic (or rather syncretistic) analysis of intervention, relating it to various fundamental values and structural factors—bureaucratic mechanisms, motives, and recruitment patterns; capitalism and its peculiar economic and organizational incentives; and political sociology and the manipulation of symbols and information by the Executive.

3. Chapter 4.

Chapter 9. The Ultimate Strategic Lessons

1. Of course, strategy connotes implementation; and national strategy stands in relation to foreign policy as military strategy to national strategy, and tactics to military strategy. At each level, one activity supplies the *how* to the *what* of another activity.

2. For an elaboration of this theoretical perspective, see my forthcoming book, *Beyond the Balance of Power: Foreign Policy and International Order*.

3. Chapter 2.

4. Chapter 6.

5. This is not the place to make a substantive case for strategic disengagement. The semblance of such a case is made in Chapter 11. An extended argument is made in my article, "The Case for Strategic Disengagement," *Foreign Affairs*, April 1973. It is enough here to put forward a strategic critique of the foreign and military policies of the recent past and to cite those features of the present situation that might discourage the hope that our foreign policy will be remedied by better instruments, or more proportional or selective responses, or attention to priorities, or moral regeneration and social reconstruction.

6. The phrase appears in Daniel Ellsberg, *Papers on the War* (New York:

Simon and Schuster, 1972), p. 238, and "Americans in Vietnam: The Lessons of My Lai," in Erwin Knoll and Judith Nies McFadden, eds., *War Crimes and the American Conscience* (New York: Holt, Rinehart and Winston, 1970), p. 128: ". . . the killing of women and children from a distance"; "high explosives from our planes and artillery." It is also the title of a book (Russell F. Weigley, *The American Way of War: A History of United States Military Strategy and Policy*, New York: Macmillan, 1973) that makes the point that, after the Civil War, the U. S. military moved from a strategy of attrition (in the strict sense) to a strategy of annihilation—the search for a climactic victory; in the context of Vietnam, "search and destroy" and the bombing of the North. Stuart Symington, Secretary of the Air Force in the late 1940s, said, "If it is preferable to engage in a war of attrition, one American life for one enemy life, then we are wrong. This is not our way." (Hearings, House Committee on Armed Services, *The National Defense Program—Unification and Strategy*, 81st Congress, 1st Session, pp. 402–403.)

Chapter 10. The Logic of the Domestic and International Systems

1. Richard Holbrooke, "Pusing Sand," *New Republic*, May 3, 1975.

2. Editorial, "After Vietnam," *New York Times*, May 4, 1975.

3. Anthony Lewis, "Hubris, National and Personal," *New Republic*, May 3, 1975.

4. Joseph Kraft, "Letting Go of the Vietnam Issue," *Washington Post*, May 6, 1975. A year later, Kraft could still pen this congratulatory message: "No domino has even wobbled" ("A Year After Vietnam: The Fixation Continues," *Washington Post*, May 2, 1976).

5. Henry Brandon, *New York Times*, April 13, 1975.

6. Stanley Hoffmann, "The Sulking Giant," *New Republic*, May 3, 1975.

7. Though Secretary Kissinger, eighteen months later, would still reflect, "The impact on the perception of other countries of the American failure in Indochina will take many years to work itself out, and therefore I have to say no one should recommend to a country that losing a war is painless." (Address at Seattle, Washington, July 22, 1976, *Department of State Bulletin*, August 16, 1976, p. 228.)

8. April 11, 1975.

9. See the report of Rowland Evans and Robert Novak, "Vietnam: Autopsy of the Collapse," *Washington Post*, April 20, 1975.

10. "Our SOBs," *New Republic*, May 3, 1975.

11. Raul S. Manglapus, *Philippines: The Silenced Democracy* (Maryknoll, N.Y.: Orbis Books, 1976), pp. 1 ff.

12. *New York Times*, July 27, 1977.

13. But others' perceptions cannot be manipulated indefinitely, and our own perceptions cannot remain forever in the realm of willful self-delusion —as much of the current pseudo-cognitive theory of "images" and superstrategy of "suasion" seems to imply. The perceptions of others are not our own. And even our own perceptions are, after all, either true or false— congruent or discordant with reality. Eventually there must be a convergence.

14. Address to the New Zealand National Press Club, April 7, 1975, reported in the *Washington Post*, April 13, 1975.

15. *Washington Post*, August 29, 1976.

16. *Washington Post*, June 24, 1976.

17. In March 1976, Moshe Dayan was reported to say "that Israel must have the nuclear option because the United States can no longer police the world." (Cited in the words of C. L. Sulzberger, "Mammoth in the Swamp," *New York Times*, Op-Ed, March 24, 1976.)

18. For such a positive judgment of the efficacy of the mining of Haiphong and the Christmas 1972 bombing of Hanoi, see Gen. George J. Eade, U.S.A.F., "Reflections on Air Power in the Vietnam War," *Air University Review*, November–December 1973. But, for negative judgments on the necessity and effectiveness of these moves, see Tad Szulc, "How Kissinger Did It: Behind the Vietnam Cease-Fire Agreement," *Foreign Policy*, summer 1974.

19. Doris Kearns, "Who *Was* Lyndon Baines Johnson?" *The Atlantic*, June 1976, p. 70. Johnson and his advisors also espoused the first two rationales.

Chapter 11. Adjusting to a Second-Best World

1. Such ideas have also characterized the program of the Trilateral Commission, a nongovernmental association of policy-oriented politicians, former government officials, business executives, and academics from North America, Western Europe, and Japan, of which a significant number of high office holders of the Carter administration have been members (including the President himself, his Secretary of State, and his National Security Advisor, Zbigniew Brzezinski. Brzezinski has characterized some of the options for our international politics in his own way (in "U. S. Foreign Policy: The Search for Focus," *Foreign Affairs*, July 1973). A balance of power policy and managed interdependence would correspond, very roughly, to Brzezinski's categories of "power realism" and "planetary humanism." Brzezinski's own preference has often been identified with the alternative of alliance and moralism. The alternative to all the above policies, which I describe as strategic disengagement, Brzezinski loosely dismisses as "introversion." A reasoned case for managed interdependence is Miriam Camps, *The Management of Interdependence: A Preliminary View* (New York: Council on Foreign Relations, 1974).

2. See the articles of Thomas L. Hughes, "Liberals, Populists, and Foreign Policy," *Foreign Policy*, fall 1975; and Richard H. Ullman, "The 'Foreign World' and Ourselves: Washington, Wilson, and the Democrat's Dilemma," *Foreign Policy*, winter 1975–76.